Moonshine

Fear and Overcoming It

Grant Burris

Great Legacy Productions
Costa Mesa, California

Grant Burris/Great Legacy Productions
1601 Sandalwood St.
Costa Mesa, CA 92626
www.moonshinebook1.com

Publisher's Note: This is a work of fiction. Names, characters, places, and incidents are a product of the author's imagination. Locales and public names are sometimes used for atmospheric purposes. Any resemblance to actual people, living or dead, or to businesses, companies, events, institutions, or locales is completely coincidental.

Book Layout ©2013 BookDesignTemplates.com

Ordering Information:
Quantity sales. Special discounts are available on quantity purchases by corporations, associations, and others. For details, contact the "Special Sales Department" at the address above.

Moonshine/Grant Burris -- 1st ed.
ISBN 978-0-9966282-0-4

Dedicated to all abused kids

No matter how you feel, get up, dress up,
show up
and
Never give up.

Zig Ziglar

Introduction

I mention the following due to my compulsion to justify the motive of my essay. At first lightly and later in life, dynamically, I've felt the emotional development of me as a young man and those items that, figuratively, tempered my steel, could be useful to another individual if I could only lay them out in an easily understood manner. I have tried to perform that to the best of my ability on the following pages. Beyond the chronicle of affairs that I will attempt in the following pages, I have a message. My message to the reader, "There's much more to a Life than the adolescent preamble to adulthood." Take from your growth years what you can use. Throw the unpleasant memories into the trash. Life is a continual process of selecting which luggage one must set down before continuing the journey. I will illustrate that. In the following chapters is a brief summary of what I became and what I sat down following the Whisky experiences.

If I have virtues, two are: Work hard. Study hard. The accumulation of knowledge is vital. Those traits were learned while life around me was secretive and challenging. '*Survive*' and '*Learn*' were lessons pounded into me early. *Survive* usually equates with *Learning* quickly. Both are valid instructions. As a result of the shared relationship of those lessons, most things I do are done with a certain gusto including those times when I rest. Work hard. Play hard. Rest hard. The last statement sounds contradictory, at first. It's not. 'Rest hard' means simply to rest completely rather than trying to do a few things *while* resting. I believe things worth doing should be performed at wide open throttle. Races on the track or competition in life can only be won by aggressive application of the throttle. One can expect less than stellar results when entering events of life where the strategy is less than full application of the throttle.

I have three children. Now, two ladies and a man. Tammy, Dawn and Jason in that order. Tammy and Dawn have a different mother than Jason. Tammy, the oldest, will always occupy the top spot by virtue of birth date and living through childbirth. There was a boy nearly a year before Tammy but he survived only the initial hours after his premature burst onto life's stage. His death changed his mother forever. Her perpetual smile faded to a frown and worse. The place where smiles are born scabbed over, then scarred, permanently. His birth, his life, his death, brief as it was, became a lesson that modified my thinking on deep levels such as: Why are we here? Mostly, I said, silently over and over, why did this death happen? Why? Painful as it was, I accepted it better than his mother. Perhaps I kept the emotions better hidden. I have tried to grasp the magnitude of emotions that must set up residence when one gives life to another then looses that life. It's a place only Mothers can know. Mothers who send sons and daughters to wars must feel this unique emotion upon their departure..... and perhaps long afterwards.

Dawn was born with her unique and sensitive personality. Her heart is forever on her sleeve. Following Tammy and before Dawn was another son, stillborn. Why? Jason was born eight years later, following Dawn, well into my second marriage. In the lives of parents, the births of kids are always milestones.

As I grew up I had many rules to which I was forced to adhere. They were tough rules. Among them was to never give up, no matter what. That premise was sound. The following essay pertains to a particular segment of my growing. I am, repeatedly, determined to illustrate a lesson learned. Summed, that lesson is: *Nothing is all bad or all good. Secret* things are not always *dishonest* things. Good can be found in bad situations if one looks carefully. I have learned to search for the *good* as a result of my experiences during the period discussed in this essay. I have never abandoned the search for *good* within *bad* situations. From the title you may have assumed this essay is about Whisky. It isn't. It is about fear and overcoming it. Many of my core philosophies sprouted during this era. They reached maturity of thinking as I reached maturity. I continue to grow.

Preface

***"There are three kinds of stories. There are stories that you want to tell, stories that you need to tell and stories that you will never tell."* Grant Burris**

The earliest forms of storytelling were thought to have been primarily oral, combined with gestures and vocal expressions. In addition to being part of religious rituals, rock art may have been a form of storytelling for many ancient cultures. The Aboriginal people of Australia painted symbols from stories upon cave walls. It was a means of helping the storyteller remember the story. Think of it as an ancient whiteboard. The 'story' was then told using a combination of oral narrative, music, rock art and dance. People have used the carved trunks of living trees and ephemeral media (such as sand and leaves) to record stories in pictures or with a combination of it and writing. Complex forms of tattooing may also represent stories, with information about genealogy, affiliation and social status.

With the dawn of writing and the use of stable, portable media, stories were recorded, transcribed and common over wide regions of the world. Stories have been carved, scratched, painted, printed or inked onto wood or bamboo, ivory and other bones, pottery, clay tablets, stone, palm-leaf books, skins, bark cloth, paper, silk, canvas and other textiles, recorded on film, and stored electronically in digital form. We even sent a story into space. Oral stories continue to be committed to memory and passed from generation to generation, despite the increasing popularity of written and televised media in much of the world. The following story was neither oral nor written until now. This story was stored in my memory instead of a memory chip. Perhaps, with luck, it too will be scratched on a cave wall someday with appropriate illustrative gestures to embellish it.

I have decided there are three kinds of stories. There are stories that you want to tell, stories that you need to tell and stories that you will never tell.

I was trained to never tell the one that follows. I was sworn to secrecy and punished with beatings when it seemed I had not obeyed the code that was branded into me. Over time, I began to want to tell the story. The *'want'* burned and festered within me but I would not break that early code. Fear is a great tutor. Secrecy had been baptized into me. Early, during the construction of my rough draft, I realized how badly I 'needed' to tell it. I had been holding it in too long.

So.... this story qualifies as an entrant in all three categories. It is nonfiction. All of it happened. There are no embellishments. I assumed my literary liberty and spared the reader some of the profanity, actually, a lot of the profanity, by sacrificing it when I thought the inclusion added little or nothing to the story. You'll recognize those places when you get to them.

Perhaps I was inspired to leave the profane on the table because I had once read and been inspired by Jack London's tale, ***"Sea Wolf"***. London, whose style I admire, composed a novel of adverse times filled with tough characters on board a ship at sea. ***Sea Wolf*** mirrored much of London's early life. The unsavory characters on board and their activities comprised 366 pages with nary a word of profanity. I decided, after reading my 110 year old original publication of this novel, that London was a genius with a capability of describing rowdy scenes accurately without the requirement for profane language. Remarkable. As I read it, I imagined the cast of characters were spewing the most vile interpretations of blasphemous speech. Yet, there was not an instance of it on any page. I was impressed. So... I followed London's lesson. Within these pages, I edited some of the profanity. If you miss it, consider this: I was showing respect for Mr. London.

Contents

CHAPTER ONE

Sand Road

You could fire a shotgun in the front door and out the back without touching a wall.

That's a shotgun house.

Events occur repetitiously in one's life. Those events have a way of embedding themselves into your memory, hiding and taking up residence within your subconscious whether you like it or not. In this instance, that applies to me. Because of that 'Truth', the mention of a single word triggers the projection of a picture into my conscious mind like one had pressed the 'Play' button on a digital recorder. For me, that key word is *Moonshine*. The mention of it signals a parade of images through my brain. Some of the images are nice. Some are not. I was born into a family that made and sold whisky. My Father made it in the woods and sold it in town. Like it or not, I was along for the ride.

A dominant image set materializes when I recall my life in a moonshine family. It is a frame set that originates during a period when I was a small, bored kid with few expectations and much less for entertainment. Mentally, the images begin rolling like a B movie in a cheap theater. I believe I can faintly smell the popcorn. In those images, I'm sitting in a hot car with the window down waiting for my dad to negotiate a sale with a potential whisky buyer. In this scene, my age is about 9 or 10. The scene was frequent and familiar. It's Arkansas summertime on a dirt road. For those who are unfamiliar with the classic southern climate, that means hot, humid and sweaty. The road is named the Sand Road, because it is. I'm sitting in front of a row house that is alongside another row house sometimes called a 'Shotgun'. I can smell the weeds. I can smell the dogs. They make their home under the porch. I can smell my own sweat. My personal odor deepens depending on how long I'd been sitting there in the sunshine in the car waiting for Alva to talk to the buyer. Alva was my dad. And, he had always been 'Alva', never 'Dad'. The handle was his preference since before I could remember. I'm still puzzled by his choice of his name rather than the traditional 'Dad'. Perhaps he was in denial that I was his son. That thought was not lost on me. That 'buyer' was consistently black. The buyer always seemed to live in a ram-shackled old house located in a poor part of town. This one fit the pattern. The house in this image was the style known as the 'Shotgun'. That meant the rooms, two or three, were all in a row. Sometimes several houses of this type of were erected side by side from the same plans. Always, poor people lived in them.

Throughout the south, 'Shotguns' were constructed for sharecroppers. Here, there were no sharecroppers. There were no crops. Just destitute people living in run down houses. Often they paid no rent. They lived from one welfare check to the next. And, they barely lived. They were lucky to have a squalid roof over their heads at night. The 'Shotguns' were simple designs and cheaply constructed. They were named appropriately. The saying was, you could fire a shotgun through all the rooms, in the front door and out the back without the blast ever hitting a wall. It would be a straight shot. Hence the name. The 'customer', especially in this case, was also likely someone that Alva had courted for a while prior to the first sale. He would often make his customer choice based on his opinion of their potential. He was customarily correct in his assumption of their latent ability to resell. Alva seemed to be forever parked in front of an old house making a deal while I sat sweating in the parked car. He was always making a deal to sell a gallon of whisky in a clear glass jug, delivered later in the moonlight.

CHAPTER TWO

Shotgun House

When someone mentions Moonshine, the image comes to me of Maggie smiling with my dad while her kids played half naked in the white sand.

Shotgun House
Long and narrow with no hallway.
The house in the story is gone. This one survived.

To cock the hammer on this particular scenario, Alva would get up from the table where he'd been sitting, at our home, on Babcock Street, in Malvern, Arkansas, wipe the sweat from his face, pick up his hat from where it hung on a nail driven into the wall, place the hat slightly off center on his head, look at me briefly and say, "I'm going over across town and see if I can sell some for tonight. You wanna' go with me? You can sit in the car while I talk to 'em. Bring that book you're reading if you want to." Then he'd stand with his head tilted to the side in a way that made the brim parallel with the floor as he stared at me, intently, and waited for my answer.

This scene is plucked from many similar scenarios and represents Alva's general theme of increasing the customer base for whisky, all the while making every attempt to choose those customers who were trustworthy and capable of keeping the secret of whisky sales combined with a personal need to improve their lot in life. Alva was discreet and very selective when he chose a new customer. Many people did not meet his criteria. Fact is, many people, beyond his customer base, failed to measure up to Alva's expectations. He had tough and proprietary standards. He had two basic types of customer. Type 1 was a person of little wealth who chose to purchase whisky and resell it a shot at a time to drinkers. Type 1 purchased and resold whisky as a small business. Sometimes, Type 1 did not consume whisky or any alcoholic beverage. Type 2 was a more affluent individual who was always a consumer of the purchased whisky. Type 2 was more connoisseur and less likely to be an alcoholic. Type 2 required that we deliver to their home, always. Type 2 was likely a Doctor, an Attorney or a successful business man. Alva had one customer who was a circuit judge in Hot Springs which was 22 miles away. The Judge's whiskey required special preparation by aging it in a charred oak keg. The lengthy aging process in the oak keg gave it a golden color and produced a product with a smooth flavor that was unforgettable. The price was more than doubled for this level of whisky. It took a considerable amount of extra time to prepare it. Plus, a portion of the quantity was absorbed by the oak keg.

'Sell some', meant, 'Sell some whisky'. Alva's ploy initiated his invitation to take a ride with him. In reality, he wanted a companion. He also expected me to be the lookout. The 'book' comment was a hook. And, of course, I always had a book half finished. Although he encouraged me to take a book, so that I'd agree to go, he preferred that I not read while he was talking. And, he was usually talking. He was forever telling one of his many stories. I would take my half finished book. However, I harbored a wish of which he was unaware. That was: Maybe he'd let me drive the car this time.

In the image that I'm thinking into existence, I accompanied Alva although I had not been allowed to drive on this trip. I sat on the passenger side, holding my book and listening to Alva tell me again how he would gladly do something else, other than "sell this whisky", if he had the education. He would run through his mind, and through mine, all the justifications for selling whisky in lieu of working at a typical daily job. As he ran it through his mind, he voiced his opinion, openly, of himself and the world. Sometimes, I wondered if he was even talking to me. He was talking more to himself than anyone. I believe that was the case. The dialogue often followed the same lines. The script was the same until we arrived at a destination. Then he'd caution me to stay in the car until he returned. That's the promise I'd made on this particular morning not unlike other mornings. I am sitting in a 1954 Chevy four door, red with a white top, on a sandy road in front of an unpainted house with no windows and only the remains of a door that likely long ago had given up it's ability to swing on it's hinges. The house is like the one in the picture only there is no grass in the front yard. Only sand and many stray dogs. It's Saturday afternoon. From the angle of the door, due to hinges broken from the wood, that door had not closed, completely, for a long time. I can see all the way through the house from my viewing angle where

I sit in the car. It's a 'Shotgun House'. Built cheap. Narrow, with all the rooms in a row. It was low quality when new. It is lower quality now. The weather-beaten wood appears to have never been blessed with a coat of paint. Never will it likely see paint and a brush. Robbed of its wheels, the carcass of a car body sits nearby flat on the sand with little of the original paint remaining. I can't remember the manufacturer. The car's original finish had been a reddish brown that, now in it's swan song of oxidation, blends perfectly with the rust that is invading its metal real estate. The rust, unwittingly, seems to be making a futile attempt to color- match the manufacturer's original finish. The stain of the rusting hulk and a few random scrub bushes are the only items landscaping the white sand around the dilapidated tenement style house. The scene of the house, the car and the family of kids running around is like the sharecroppers right out of the movie, ***Grapes of Wrath***. Alva's foot makes the steps creak as he puts his weight on them. The steps angle to one side like the door. The hollow sound of his shoe heels on the wooden floor as he enters reminds me of how empty the house is of furniture and the absence of the customary personal items that dampen the sound in most homes. Compared to my home, we were poor, but at least we had furniture and personal items in the house. Standing in the inner doorway that connects the two rooms is a tall thin Black woman. Alva addresses her as Maggie. Her dress is so thin that I can see the silhouette of her taunt black body right through the thin white cloth. It's easy to detect that she's wearing nothing underneath. I can't help staring. Her charcoal black skin and the backlighting from the open back door makes it easier to detect the body's subtle shape. Alva knows Maggie. She seems glad to see him based on her smile. She's about 30 - 35. Her teeth, with an exaggerated overbite that compliments her face with a perpetual smile, and her eyes, are all I can see of her face in that back-lighted posture standing there in the doorway of her Shotgun house on Saturday afternoon on the old Sand Road. Alva is relaxed under these conditions as he conducts his whisky negotiations with Maggie. He feels comfortable here. You can detect it in his speech and it's telegraphed by his body movements.

Running around the yard, playing simple games that are a cross between tag and dodge ball, is no fewer than 15 kids whose extremely black skin contrasts with the bleached white sand. There must be a correlation between one's financial condition and fertility. All the poor people had a house full of kids. These kids are easy to see because they stand out so from the sand. The contrast is incredible. The sand at this location is whiter than anywhere nearby. I have no justification for this geological anomaly. Most of the local sandy spots have amber sand. For whatever geographical reason this area contains sand that is noticeably very white. I noticed and pondered that characteristic each time I visited this spot. Everything with color seems exaggerated. The sand is lighter here and the kids are blacker. Adding to the richness of their color, they seemed to never sweat when they play. I noticed that repeatedly and wondered, why? Their skin is flat black like charcoal without the shine of perspiration. They are all skinny as rails. I'm puzzled by their physical features. Is it a genetic trait or is it lack of nutrition? It's likely a combination. They look like clones except for their height. Each one appears exactly like the next. They are like stair steps. No two are the same height. Occasionally, when one of their paths, in the improvised game, takes them near the Chevrolet where I sit, they snap a glance in my direction with only their eyes and no head movement. They flick their glance toward me like an optical whip as they manage their game in such a way that it becomes a round robin routine giving each a chance to glance in my direction as they pass without revealing a direct stare. They are as curious about me as I am about them. Many of them, especially the smallest ones, who are three feet high and shorter, have no clothes. They are as naked as freshly hatched birds. At least half of the group is without clothes and, seemingly, oblivious to a dress code. All are barefooted. The ones with clothes only have on the barest of necessities which hides less than it should on the girls. None are wearing underwear beneath their tattered dresses. Now, as I think about it with many years added to my perspective, I'll wager most of them had never owned a pair of shoes. Of those who had, they were likely hand me downs from an older sibling or friend who had outgrown the item. I noticed one boy, maybe 12 years old. He has shoes but the two don't match. He doesn't care. The shoes have no laces. The normally vertical portion above the heel is flattened by long days underneath his heel. It has been converted into a slip-on loafer and will wear for a while after he has out grown it. The kids speak English but I can seldom understand a word. It's not my English. Their slang combined with the broken grammar transposes what they are speaking into a language all new and impossible for me to understand other than a few snatches here and there. I listen, nevertheless, without appearing to. I have my book as a prop. During their game, sometimes, they fall. The screams from pain are universal, I suppose.

Alva is already inside the small shotgun house, talking to the mother. It's another stop. It's another deal. There is little doubt that the woman to whom Alva is speaking is the mother of the brood I'm watching. The kids, even the smallest ones, are perfect images of the Mom. Obviously, the kids, all of them, are her offspring. She is tall, very black and has prominent teeth that seem to be exposed a lot when she talks. That is especially true of her upper teeth. She has that severe overbite. I am young and naive but not so much so that I think all black people look alike. After all, due to Alva's preference of customers, I have been associated with the black community and black folks all my life.

That image of the kids in their perpetual game is a common one if I allow myself to dream of those times as I am now. When someone mentions Moonshine, the image comes to me of Maggie smiling with my dad while her kids played half naked in the white sand.

It's easy to remember the grinning black lady and the kids who lived in the shotgun on the Sand Road. The family at this little house followed a strong genetic trait. They all appeared amazingly related. Both boys and girls had a similar appearance. Later, I learned, based on those physical features, they were likely of Namibian origin. Upon recalling this period later, I remember never seeing a father figure at the house. This fact failed to strike me as unusual. Black men were often absent from the home when we paid a visit. Absent, at least to the sight. Sometimes, the man was there but asleep in a back room. Often, they were truly missing in action. It was not uncommon for black men to abandon their offspring when they were not married. Black men frequently had offspring at several households within a given area. It was common for the lady of the house to be the single parent and the bread winner. The absence of a father figure became one of the key points of this episode later as Alva attempted and succeeded in teaching

Maggie how to earn and manage her money. The Maggie and children model was typical of the customers Alva courted regularly. They made solid customers and they were trustworthy. They were goal oriented and Alva appreciated and enhanced that quality within them.

I'm getting ahead of the story, deliberately. But I'll come back to it later. That scene of the black kids on the white sand always stuck with me and still does. The starkness of the extreme black on the extreme white of the sand was a metaphor for the contrast found within the ethics of the moonshine business. So much of the whisky business was illegal and so much of it seemed commendable. To wax philosophical, some things are illegal because they are bad. Some things are bad because they are illegal. The illegal whisky industry was a bit of each. The violent contrast, the simultaneous good and the bad of the business was a metaphor for my father's life and his personal values. Often very forgettable and memorable events were occurring as one. It took me many years to assimilate myself into the double standard of the work. Later, it took many years to extract myself from the memories. As I write about it, the feelings return but not with the magnitude I experienced when young. Now, it's as though all of it had happened to someone else whose life I had the unique privilege to closely observe.

CHAPTER THREE

Wet and Dry

Whether it is good, bad, first or last is a matter of one's perspective.

Early in my life, as a Moonshiner's son, I had become acquainted with the dual roles one must assume when engaged in the distillation and sale of whiskey. I learned early that when Alva said there was nothing wrong with making and selling whisky, there was a lot wrong with talking about it or discussing his activities with an outsider. That was difficult for me to comprehend when I was small. A few 'lessons' with his leather belt taught me a lot. (that 'leather belt' was a 3 inch wide double sharpening strop for an open razor) I would frequently break into a sweat at the sight of him unrolling that belt after he removed it from a shaving box where it was kept. The fear caused a strange taste in my mouth as I watched him prepare to administer a 'lesson'. I would clamp my jaws together, stiffen my neck and wish for it to be over. Always, I tried to endure it without crying. Always, I failed. Toward the end I would loose my composure. The dual ethics of the trade did not always run parallel. You will see what I mean as I explain more of it.

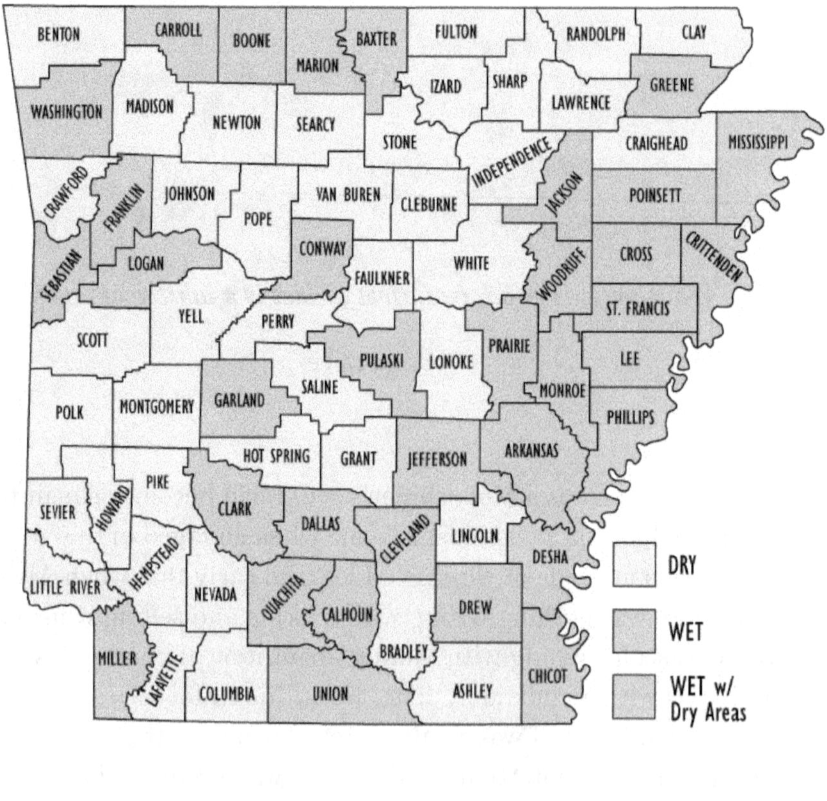

I grew up in Arkansas. There are 75 counties in the state. Each one, depending on the influence of the local churches in that particular county, voted on whether that county would be 'dry' or 'wet'. Dry was defined as follows: no sale of alcoholic beverages allowed within the boundary of the county. Wet, of course meant the opposite. One could sell properly taxed and regulated whiskey, known in the circles as 'bottled and bond' or store bought whisky, within that 'wet' county if the store was fully licensed to do so and in possession of a Liquor License. There are a few counties that were 'wet' but with restrictions on specific areas within that county. It was a bit confusing. It was common to see a sign on the roadside announcing that one was leaving a dry county. The sign, depending on direction of travel, reminded the traveler of what he must be thinking, that this would be the first or last opportunity to purchase legally merchandised whisky. The store owner capitalized on that thought with the name of the business. At a roadside just inside the county line of a wet county was often a 'honky tonk' bar with vehicles parked around it on the gravel. The cars, especially if they were at the edge of the parking area, often contained a couple engaged in promiscuous behavior. In the summer, the car windows would be down, and the moans of passion from back seat were as loud as the ever present jukebox that could be heard throughout the parking area and beyond. The sign, the name of the bar on the side facing the dry county was 'First Chance'. On the side viewed by those leaving the wet county was 'Last Chance'. I remember a honky tonk just like this that we passed each time we drove between Malvern and Hot Springs on highway 270. Half way between the two towns was the county line. The county line separated the dry county, Hot Spring, from the wet county, Garland. (Don't confuse Hot Spring, the county, with Hot Springs, the city). The honky-tonk bar was just inside the Garland county (wet county) line.

As we traveled north toward Hot Springs the sign read, *First Chance*. As we traveled the opposite direction from Hot Springs toward Malvern the sign read, *Last Chance*. Good old Last Chance, First Chance. It just depended on which way you were traveling. Life is somewhat the same. Whether it is good, bad, first or last is a matter of one's perspective. All depends on which direction your mind is pointed. Moonshine whiskey has a similar pedigree too. I had plenty of chances to receive repeated lessons on this paradoxical topic as I grew up.

Alva was filled with metaphors and memories. It seemed that everything we passed on the road either reminded him of a previous event or opened a window into a prediction of the future. Alva once said that one could walk from Malvern to the Garland County line (wet county), about 12 miles, without touching the ground by stepping on the whiskey bottles that were thrown from cars and lying on the side of the road. That was pretty close to the truth. The roadsides between Malvern (dry) and the county line was littered with plenty of whisky and beer bottles. The density of the empty bottles increased as one approached Malvern. The spirits originally in the bottles had been purchased at good old *Last Chance*, or a similar place, by Malvern residents and consumed on the way back home. The bottle had to be tossed before arriving home, of course. So, out the window it went. Alva was filled with euphemisms that hinged on earned truth. He more than once revealed his belief that the same church members who always voted our county, Hot Spring County, dry, were the very people who drank more whiskey than anyone else. The group who threw the empties on the roadside was likely heavily populated by those Alva scorned with his remarks.

He once said, "They vote to keep Hot Spring county dry and then they drive to Garland County to buy whiskey. They drink it while they drive home, drunk, and throw the bottles out the window onto the shoulder of the road. Sometimes, you find one of these rascals in his car after it has wrapped it around a power pole or a tree."

He always believed that the hypocritical church members consumed more whiskey than the average citizen. He was likely accurate. After all, he was a professional in the industry. He should know his facts better than most. He sometimes sold to some of the same people who voted to keep the county dry. He would not sell to them directly. He used an intermediary. He failed to trust the "hypocrites". He often voiced his displeasure with their ethics.

"Anybody who's a hypocrite cannot be trusted. They might turn me in to the law. So, I don't want them to ever see me selling directly to them."

He'd often elaborate on it until he grew tired of the subject.

It was common to hear him say, "I'd trust a damn drunk before I'd trust a member of a church who has proven to be a hypocrite." He'd continue with a chuckle, "Of course, most of those hypocrites I'm talking about..... are damn drunks."

Whisky, or moonshine, distilled by individuals privately was always unlawful to manufacture, possess or sell. The Moonshiner makes it. The Bootlegger sells it. My dad was often both.

Alva would say as a reflection, "They're always trying to catch me. So far, they haven't succeeded. That makes 'em mad." Then he would put on a slight smile as he glanced in my direction. He reveled in his cunning techniques while always remembering that he could easily die from a police bullet as had his brother.

Many laws were structured around the manufacture and sale of untaxed liquor. Untaxed liquor was simply the formal name for moonshine whiskey. The state law makers didn't care if you drank it or not. The government didn't give a hoot about the purity or the alcohol content. Not really. They simply wanted the tax revenue. Don't believe rumors to the effect that the government was trying to protect people from "All that improperly made product". The toxic content of the moonshine whisky was the most distant thing from law enforcement's mind. All else beyond the monetary aspect was a ruse to appease the ignorant and the religious community. At the local level, the police wanted their "shake down money". They were unafraid to make the requests for a pay off. I'll get to that later.

Individuals who wanted to distill their own whiskey or spirits have always found ways to do it secretly without the awareness of the law. John Barleycorn is always trying to evade John Law. Some were more successful at the secret production of spirits than others. Sometimes the most tasty products were produced by individuals in small batches on a creek in the woods. The type of water used and the various minerals in that particular stream created an individual personality to each run of whisky. When properly performed, those nuisances of minerals in the rural streams created very attractive differences in the taste of different spirits. A good distiller, known herein as a moonshiner, could tell the difference. Alva had a sensitive palate not unlike those who discern the subtleness of wine. In the autumn of his moonshine career, when he had stopped distilling and only purchased from other distillers for resale, he always tasted prior to purchase and then again upon delivery to make sure he was receiving what he had ordered. I've seen him reject a load of whiskey with a shake of his head and a second taste that he swished in his mouth then spat on the ground.

He'd swear at no one in particular, pause for a long moment and quietly say, "That's not what I bought. Take it back."

The driver of the load never argued. They were familiar with the quickness of Alva's anger if confronted. They also were aware of my presence in the shadows with a 12 gauge and a Colt automatic pistol. Mr. Colt and Mr. Lefebvre added a note of finality to Alva's demand. The load would be returned, at great risk to the driver. Alva would retest on the following day at the point of origin. Apologies would be made and a second load would be sent. Tasting was performed as before upon deliver and the load was accepted.

"You can never put the spilled milk back into the bottle."

When the temperance movement, inspired by the churches, made the production or sale of alcoholic beverages illegal with the passage of the Eighteenth Amendment, January 17th, 1920, they simultaneously created a market for moonshine that had never existed previously. Sometimes what looks good on paper is just the opposite in real life. That was true in this case. The Eighteenth Amendment, that turned the private and commercial production of whisky, illegal, caused more strife than the whisky production, whose demise, the law was intended to promote.

Another of Alva's euphemisms: "When the temperance movement made the sale of alcohol illegal, all it did was turn average people into moonshiners and bootleggers. It closed the saloons. The closure of those establishments took the whores out of the saloons and put them on the street. When the saloons closed, the whores had no where to go except the street."

Alva said, "Never, before the temperance movement, did you see whores hanging out on the street corners trying to do their business. They stayed in the saloons where they belonged. When the saloons closed, the world's oldest profession was forced onto the street. The streets of Hot Springs, Arkansas was suddenly lined with whores. It was the same in other cites, I'm sure."

He quickly continued, "Then, with the whores on the street, respectable women began admiring them and imitating them in dress and behavior. Forever after that, men couldn't tell the difference between a whore and a respectable woman. They began to look the same and dress the same. They were all on the street together. Life has never been the same since."

In retrospect he said, "It's been hell for men every since because all the regular women began behaving like whores."

He was on a rant. On he went, "There became more broken homes than ever before. Divorces increased and more little kids were left without the benefit of two parents. And, it all traces it's roots back to the lovely Temperance Movement and the Eighteenth Amendment, that the churches preached and paraded into existence with their signs and slogans. It was the Eighteenth Amendment, to the Constitution. Thank God they repealed it after a few years. Unfortunately, you can never return things to the way they were. You can never put the spilled milk back in the bottle."

He'd shake is head slowly and get a far away look in his eyes like he was following the action of a movie from a great distance.

Then he'd shake his head again and say, "And the hypocritical sons of bitches damn me for making and selling whisky."

CHAPTER FOUR

Whisky - Hot Springs

"Anything and everything is available for a price."

When something is illegal, that automatically creates an opening for the black market. Making a product illegal simply opens up a business opportunity for those enterprising souls who know of a source for the illegal product. Al Capone and others like him, made a fortune by procuring and selling moonshine whiskey during the temperance movement. Capone bought the protection of law enforcement and utilized large stills to produce whiskey in and near Hot Springs, Arkansas. Capone was a bootlegger not a moonshiner. Capone never made an ounce of whisky.

Mountain Valley Water
Central Avenue, Hot Springs, Arkansas

He sold and required such quantities of it that he was required to ship it north to Chicago and his speakeasies in tank cars by way of the railroad. The requirements must have been enormous. The whiskey was put into the rail cars. The railcars were labeled "Mountain Valley Water" which was the name of a local and legitimate mineral spring water company. Whether Mountain Valley Water was in on the deal or not is unknown. Rumor says they were but I wouldn't want to imply that the rumor was true. Capone would not have hesitated to plagiarize the name. He did far worse during his career. That part is unknown but rumors still persist.

Hot Springs, Arkansas had a fledgling industry of mineral water that was and still is widely known. The mineral water fit nicely into the historical image of Hot Springs and it's bathhouse row where hot artesian mineral water sprang from the ground 24 hours a day. Hot Springs had both hot artesian water and mineral water from springs that came out of the ground normal temperature. Capone capitalized on Mountain Valley Water, a name that was well known. The whiskey was shipped to Chicago under the guise of mineral water from world famous Hot Springs. This was one operation that I was familiar with because my dad explained it to me. When I was small he showed me the places where the massive quantities of whiskey was brewed for Capone. He knew many of the 'makers'. Some of those 'makers', later, after Capone was gone, became suppliers for Alva, on a much smaller scale, after Alva, personally, abandoned the making of whisky. Fifty years later I read about Capone's activities while revisiting Hot Springs. The reports collaborated Alva's stories. The hushed whispers of Capone's activity in and around Hot Springs during those early years has become the lore of books today. It all happened. As a sidebar to that: Capone was never prosecuted for marketing illegal alcohol. Capone was imprisoned for tax fraud. He was not executed. He ultimately died from gonorrhea that he contracted from one of his call girls. The popular story regarding Capone's ability to elude police so easily was: He bribed the local police. That theory, if true, shows that crime, big crime, does pay if one is capable of 'buying' corrupt law enforcement personnel. We hear of this happening with regularity. So, it is likely true in the case of Capone.

Alva used to say, "Anything and everything is available for a price." He should have known. I've heard the police ask him directly to pay them for their protection. I'll explain that to you later.

CHAPTER FIVE

Small Moonshiners

I miss those happy scraps, those rations of laughter that slip through my memory like a wisp of blue smoke in the tree tops from an oak fire under a moonshiner's still.

Many small operators, backwoods alchemists, moonshiners if you will, made a living for their families by making and selling small quantities of moonshine whiskey. Capone not only paid the law enforcement to protect his operation. He paid them to chase and apprehend his competitors as well. So, if you were a small time operator you had to avoid the discovery of Capone and the police as well as your competitors. Some small operators were clever and were able to avoid both Capone and the police. They were successful to a degree. Others were not so lucky. They are buried in unmarked graves.

Running a still to make some whisky was frequently only an alternative job akin to the flipping of burgers today when one is unable to find regular work. When one's formal education prevented the acquisition of a regular job, you could always make and sell a little whiskey if you could find a good creek in the woods where no one was likely to stumble on it. Then, came the challenge of avoiding discovery and capture. To achieve secrecy, one was required, first, to suspend all talk regarding it. In addition, the path to the still must be different each time the still is visited so that a trail is never formed. With the best of location, one could perform only one, perhaps two runs at a location before relocating. Last, one required the knowledge of the ingredients and the process of distillation. The physical work during set up, distillation and distribution to hiding spots for the finished product was enormous. Making whisky was not easy. It was a hard sweaty job that was often performed at night with only moonlight for illumination.

It was not unusual to hear one of the locals say, "I can't find any work. I've been thinking about making a little whisky for a while 'till I find something to do." Those making open comments such as that were normally the first to be apprehended by police.

Making whisky was always a good fall-back-to job if other opportunities evaporated as they frequently did for uneducated individuals.

The name 'Moonshine' was derived by the fact that often it was necessary to distill it or what was referred to by still operators as "make a run", during night time by no light other than the moon light. My dad was one of those Moonshiners. Alva was many things. He was versatile but he was definitely a Moonshiner. He was one of those home spun chemical engineers who had remembered well the lessons, totally verbal, which had been handed down from older members of the family. Although he usually made his still runs during daylight, he often carried the still components to and from locations during the dead of night in a traditional and mandatory manner. He made his preparations well. He'd read the Farmer's Almanac to determine when the moon was going to be full. Then, he'd schedule his carrying expedition, usually single handed, to coincide with the full moon. Often individual components, like the pot for boiling the mash, weighed over 200 pounds. Each individual wooden barrel used for brewing the mash (he used six) weighed about 100 pounds. Each of these items required a separate trip, a different path, to the still site. The very nature of the secrecy demanded that the heavy pot and all other items be carried on his shoulders, in the dark, for miles into thick forest. The pot was sometimes two steel barrels welded together, end to end. The pot was the first component in the distillation process. Into it was poured the fermented mash from the buried wooden barrels. The big fitting for the cap, the area where the vaporized spirits came out, was welded on the side at the middle. That gave it the crude appearance of a "T" with a shortened stem. It was usually soot covered on the outside from previous wood fires used to heat the mixture. Sometimes, when Alva returned from a night time mission, his face would be black on one side from the soot of the pot and clean on the other. My mother would always wait up for him with a meal no matter how late. That meant I was often awake also, even though I'd been told to go to sleep. If I was still awake and if I saw him I'd laugh because he looked like he had makeup on one side of his face often including exactly half of his nose as though it had been skillfully applied. It gave him an unusual clown like appearance.

His clothes would be soot covered from carrying the black pot on his shoulder and when I laughed he would smile and say, "What's the matter? What are you laughing about?"

I'd say, "Look in the mirror."

He'd look and then, although he was tired, sweaty and out of breath from all the struggling through the woods, he'd begin laughing too. He would turn one way exposing one side then the other way. Then he would pretend he was going to hug me and get me all sooty too. I knew it was a game, but I'd run and he'd chase me briefly around the interior of the old one-roomed school house where we lived.

My Mom would laugh as she watched. Alva would laugh. Infrequently, did we all laugh as one. Now, I can remember those scraps of time when all was happy for a bit. I miss those happy scraps, those rations of laughter that slip through my memory like a wisp of blue smoke in the tree tops from an oak fire under a moonshiner's still.

CHAPTER SIX

Charlie - Squirrel Hunter

Charlie had keen eyesight to match his marksmanship

Alva was a great story teller. He read and wrote slowly like one would expect from a man who only completed the fourth grade. He made up for it with his ability to remember events, perfectly, and in his way of observing and including the most subtle and meaningful actions into the story. Often, he would punctuate the stories with a related poem recited from memory, verbatim. When you listened, you felt that you were there. One of his favorite poems was "The Blue and the Gray" by Ellen H. Flagg. He had first memorized it when he was in the fourth grade. That was approximately 1907. Fifty-five years later, I listened.

It depicted two fallen civil war soldiers, one Union, one Confederate, recapping their lives and families to each other as they lay dying on the battlefield. Naturally, the stories that he liked the best, the ones closest to his heart, were told more than once. They were always the same without modifications.

One of the earliest stories I can remember was of his older brother, Charlie. Alva respected and looked to Charlie for understanding which he apparently received in abundance. Charlie was about ten years older than Alva. Charlie had a love of firearms and due to much practice, he was a great marksman. Accuracy was mandatory. One could not afford to waste scarce and costly ammunition with multiple shots at game.

Alva told of many occasions where he accompanied Charlie while squirrel hunting. The little rodents were plentiful and provided many cooking pots in Arkansas with the key ingredient. To enjoy the maximum amount of the kill meant it was important to shoot them in the head. That allowed the body to be cooked without the molestation of a bullet hole and damaged meat. "More meat for the pot" as Alva would say. During many of the squirrel hunting trips that Alva recalled, portrayed himself when he was about ten to twelve years old. He was not quite old enough to do the shooting but he knew the technique required to bag a few squirrels. The trees were tall and often the squirrel would be in the very top gathering nuts. With their sharp eyes they could detect a hunter on the ground, easily, sometimes before the hunter ever saw them. In some stories Alva and Charlie had a dog that 'treed' the squirrel saving a lot of the hunter's time staring into the tree tops. On other trips, for whatever reason, there was no dog in the story.

In those cases, one was dependent on very sharp eyes. Charlie had keen eyesight to match his marksmanship.

Alva said, "So many times Charlie would say, 'Hold still there's one in the top of that tree'".

The 'tree' was always a very tall, mature tree often over 100 feet in height.

The squirrel would always go around on the back side the tree so that he could not be seen by the hunter on the ground.

Alva said, "Charlie would say why don't you go way around the other side that tree (that he was pointing at with the squirrel in it) and shake a bush."

Alva said, "I'd go way around on the other side while Charlie just stood there motionless with that little 22 pointed up."

Alva said, "I'd find a sapling that was small enough I could shake and I'd give it a little shake. I'd hear Charlie say, "Hup. Hold it.""

The squirrel had seen the shake of the sapling and had responded by moving back around the tree within sight of Charlie. That shift of the squirrel's position gave Charlie the advantage.

Alva said, "I'd hear the single spat from that 22 and down would come Mr. Squirrel".

Alva would continue, "I never remember Charlie ever shooting twice at a squirrel. It would spiral down from that tall tree. As I ran around to where Charlie stood, I'd say to him, You shot that one in the body didn't you?"

He said Charlie would put on a twinkle of a smile and say, "Go look at his head."

Alva told me that he never retrieved one shot by Charlie that was not shot directly through the center of his head.

Alva said, "It looks like of all the ones he shot there would have been one that he hit a glancing shot or a near miss but that wasn't the case. In every case, and there were many, the shots were made into very tall virgin timber with the top of the tree swaying in the wind and the head of the squirrel about the size of a silver dollar, every last shot was in the exact center of the head as though a person had carefully placed the shot there at close range."

Arkansas Hill Country Near Hot Springs

Alva was impressed by Charlie's marksmanship. He aspired to be as good a shot as Charlie. He came close. Maybe he was equal. No matter how closely he came it would not have eroded his view of Charlie. In Alva's mind Charlie was larger than life. He put Charlie on a pedestal, certainly in marksmanship, perhaps everything, that he would never exceed.

Charlie was a squirrel hunter in the truest sense of the word. He was a marksman, teacher and provider. As a side note; historically, squirrel hunters have received deserved respect for their marksmanship through out our history. They play a rich role in our heritage. Andrew Jackson relied heavily on the marksmanship of the squirrel hunters at the Battle of New Orleans during the War of 1812. Charlie was one of those legendary squirrel hunters of the south who just never missed.

Battle of New Orleans with Old Hickory's Squirrel Hunters on the Right

CHAPTER SEVEN

Charlie making Whisky

Charlie was fast on his feet and he knew the woods well in which he had grown up

Four lawmen with a captured still

A scene played out more than once with the same script. Alva and I would be in the woods. I might have been six or seven years old. Something would trigger his memory of the following event. Then he would sit on a convenient stump and relate the details to me. It went somewhat as follows.

Charlie was probably the first of the Burris family to begin making whiskey. He began about the time the temperance movement forced the whores onto the streets. He had the typical still on a small stream in the woods. He made mostly for family and friends and sold very little, if any. He was a small operator to be sure. There was plenty of lawmen who knew the technique for making small quantities of whiskey. They knew you must operate along a small stream which provided the cooling water for the distillation process once the mash had fermented for a period and was ready to be distilled. The period that followed fermentation was better known to whiskey makers as "ready to run". That meant the mash was ready to be put into the pot and begin distillation. Lawmen, when they had the opportunity, walked these small streams in search of Moonshiners. Charlie had a still not too far from his home where he lived with his wife and child. Apparently it was discovered by lawmen. They sneaked upon Charlie while he was making a run. A whisky maker was easily apprehended at this stage because the distillation process required so much of the maker's attention. The law announced themselves, but before they could get close enough to apprehend him, Charlie ran away. At the first sound of the law, Charlie spun on his heel and ran through the woods opposite from the voice that demanded he stop and surrender. Charlie was fast on his feet and he knew the woods well in which he had grown up. He simply outran them. Easily. None of the lawmen could swear to the identity of the still operator, although the were pretty sure it was Charlie Burris.

Odds are, they were embarrassed. At least that's the way the story was told. And it was told frequently not only by the lawmen but by others, probably becoming bigger and better each time it was repeated.

Time passed and the story spread of 'Charlie who outran the cops and escaped from a still'. The police involved continued to be embarrassed by their failure. The constant telling and retelling of the story, which likely became larger and made Charlie seem bolder each time it was told, caused increased embarrassment for the lawmen involved. The local police became infatuated with the idea of apprehending Charlie. Charlie was more detached from the event than most. He was likely more removed than he should have been for he didn't waste much time starting another still in a remote part of the woods. Of course, it was on a small stream as it must be. This time the local police found it with the help of a third party who found it and relayed the information to them. They suspected it may belong to Charlie but they didn't know for sure. They had scored many failed attempts busting whiskey makers, moonshiners. Due to this, they changed techniques. Their new method hinged on the idea of hiding in wait near the still and surrounding the victim at the last minute. They planned this for the still where Charlie was to be the unsuspecting victim. They carefully distanced themselves in a nearly complete circle around the still. They hid well and allowed the path into the still to be unobstructed. They may have waited more than once.

It is unknown how many times they waited or for how long they stalked the still without Charlie showing up. Ultimately, when Charlie showed up to make a run or tend to the still in preparation to making a run, they sprang out from hiding and surrounded him. They all had drawn guns and told him to put up his hands. Charlie, filled with confidence from his previous encounter months before, sprang from the scene like a cat. He was fleet on his feet and a great marksman. He was likely able to live up to the reputation he had established for outrunning anyone in the community. Today he was unarmed. He was fleet on foot but, today, he was unable to outrun the bullet fired into his back as he ran. One of the lawmen fired a rifle into his back at close range. The proximity was so close that the flash from the gunpowder burned Charlie's shirt around the bullet hole. Some believed that he did not run. Many believed that his death was the result of a shot in the back at close range. The powder burn on his shirt would tend to verify this accusation.

Alva never forgave the Malvern police department for shooting his brother in the back. He particularly blamed a deputy who bragged of pulling the trigger.

Although Alva fully understood the illegality of what Charlie was doing, he always said, "They had no right to shoot him in the back. Even if he got away they shouldn't have shot him. Charlie had a wife and family who were dependant on him. All of them knew it."

I can remember Alva saying many times, "Making whiskey is not something they should kill people for doing. No law, anywhere, says they can kill people for making whiskey. Why, killing someone is way worse than making whisky."

Alva always believed that the police could have simply arrested Charlie later since they had identified him on the spot. Alva believed that one of the policemen in particular was responsible for the decision to shoot instead of apprehending him alive. Apparently, all of the police on the scene did not agree with what went down that day in the woods. However, a deed once done could not be undone. Some of the persons present revealed the details of the incident. The story gradually leaked. This is how Alva became aware of the those details. The policeman who shot was the only one who fired a gun. He had bragged to other men in the group that day that Charlie Burris was not going to get away again. Supposedly, he had said, "I'll shoot the bastard if he runs. I might shoot him whether he runs or not. He won't get away from me." The others in the group took this as so much bragging. Apparently the bravado was more serious than they believed.

In private moments, when we were alone and when Alva had loosened his inhibitions with a few drinks, he revealed to me that he had planned to kill the deputy who shot his brother. I think Alva, in his heart, had planned exactly what he told me. I believe he was deadly serious. I think he may have been ashamed of himself for planning to avenge his brother's murder with another murder. Alva said that shortly after the death of his brother and before he could complete his strategy as to just how he was going to do it, the deputy who shot Charlie got into an altercation with someone and that deputy was shot and killed. His death was not job related. Alva said that although he was relieved to know it was over, he felt short changed for never having avenged his brother's death. He always believed that God had taken charge of the situation and saved him from the aftermath of a murder for which he would have been charged.

Sometimes, sobbing lightly and under the influence of some of his white lightning, he would succumb to the emotions of the memory. He would tell me that he may have been shortchanged of his vengeance but was relieved that he never had to kill that deputy.

He said, "Someone else took charge of that situation and righted a wrong that had been committed. Therefore, I never had to do it. But I would have if he hadn't gotten himself killed by someone else. It was in my plans."

I understand how Alva felt for I have been to the same fork in the road and have been rescued in the same mysterious way. I'm glad that neither of us, Alva or I were permitted to travel the fork less traveled.

CHAPTER EIGHT

Alva making Whisky

He was likely more frightened of dying from starvation than from a lawman's bullet.

It is surprising to me that Alva chose to make whiskey after the culmination of the previous events that included the death of his brother, Charlie. I believe that the things he revealed to me motivated him to begin.

Departure From the Dust Bowl

When the depression hit America in first quarter of the 20th century, many families were left without means to earn a living. Farmers failed at farming largely because of the drought that hit about the same time. Many who farmed could not sell what they raised because no one had money to buy. People could not even afford the essentials. Those with families suffered the most. Families with children were the hardest hit. Books, many books reveal the plight of starving families on the road looking for work of any kind just so they could survive. Alva told me of trips that he made to several areas. His were mostly futile trips because people were already there with the same problem. Alva told of purchasing a small truck that he used to do light hauling. He made meager wages because most folks had no money to pay.

They were all in the same financial condition. When the truck broke he had no money to repair it. He had a wife and two small girls. It was his first marriage and his first children. As a last and desperate attempt to earn more, he and his family decided to go to California and seek work where they had heard jobs were more plentiful. To say they were not alone with this idea was to greatly oversimplify it. Millions had similar thoughts and acted on it. The road was often littered with the carcasses of broken cars and personal belongings.

Headed West

It was little better in California. There were more jobs but also more people. There was likely more skilled people seeking jobs also. There was surely more skilled workers than in Arkansas.

In any event, the trip was not as fruitful as it had been described. Lots of people had headed west for work. Few had found their dream amongst the labor camps, empty cans, starved dogs and worn out automobiles. There were thousands of good people, hungry people, all hunting for work. At the proverbial end of the rope and needing work badly, Alva and his wife, Violet, resorted to seeking work in a farm labor camp. The only thing available was work on a huge cotton farm. They began picking cotton daily. It was the lowest form of work but it paid, badly needed, money.

Alva described how they left the two girls, Margaret and Leona, ages two and four at the end of a row in the field. He and Violet would pick to the end of the row and pick the two rows back to where the girls were. They would move the girls over two rows, then pick to the end and back again. This continued through out the day. All day, everyday, for many days they continued this.

Violet and Alva Burris February 1918
Shortly after they were married

Alva said they received for pay \$1.50 per hundred pounds of cotton picked. He said an average picker could pick 100 pounds per day. Between the two of them, although he picked slightly more than Violet, they averaged about 200 pounds per day. That's \$3.00 a day for a family of four. Alva said that when they began this job he looked in his pocket to see how much money he had. He had one dime. Alva demonstrated to me how he held that single dime in his hand. Tears would come to his eyes as he recalled the memory. He said that he looked at that dime for a long time. He thought about all the responsibility heaped upon him and he with only a dime to satisfy that load. He had only one dime to feed a family. He told me this through the tears in his eyes and made the image so vivid that I felt as though I'd seen it.

Typical Destitute Families on the Road

Kids Faired Poorly

Mothers Deeply Concerned without Choices

He said, " I looked at that dime a long time. I thought, here I am with only ten cents to my name after all I've done. I promised myself that I would do anything, anything to accumulate some money for my family. So, I thought, we will pick a little cotton since there is nothing else to do. Maybe we can accumulate enough money to get us back home."

Whole Families Picking Cotton
Often it was the only work available

He said, "I knew if I could get back to Arkansas I was going to try making some whisky, as dangerous as it was, just to get ahead a little bit."

Alva knew how to make whisky. Although he never voiced it, I believe he hesitated to begin due to fear he would wind up shot in the back like his brother. I'm convinced he was determined to support his family. He put that responsibility uppermost. Alva had the responsibilities of a father drilled into him by the fruitless trip to California and the farm labor camps overwhelmed by destitute families such as his own. He was healthy and able bodied but unable to find sufficient work to support his family. He revealed that frustration to me frequently in those stump-side sessions in the woods when he would pause for a minute to rest after carrying whisky still parts through the forest. He'd shed a few tears as he recounted the story I'm revealing here. His determination was constant and overwhelming. The frustration at the situation was equal. He was likely frightened of the prospect of moonshining, but more frightened of the absence of wealth. He was likely more frightened of dying from starvation than from a lawman's bullet.

With a few dollars earned from picking cotton, Alva and Violet and Margaret and Leona slowly made their way back to Arkansas. Alva said he managed to get a old house to live in near Hot Springs and had just enough money to buy some sugar and some corn chops after buying a meager food supply. Chops are corn kernels chopped into smaller pieces. Chops begin the fermentation process more quickly than whole kernels of corn. He found a place where he could bury the barrels needed for fermenting the mash. He dug a hole in the ground, made up the mash carefully, put the barrels in the ground, then put the mash into the buried barrels. He covered the barrels with limbs from trees and then placed leaves over them so that livestock, mainly wild pigs, would not get into the mash and drink it. He gathered enough copper pipes for routing the steam from the pot to the cooling barrel. This copper pipe is usually about two inches in diameter. Somewhere, he forgot from where, he gathered enough small copper tubing to make the 'worm' for the cooling barrel. The worm was a spiral of several feet of copper tubing placed in a barrel of re-circulated cold water. Inside the worm the mash steam, from the slowly boiling pot, was cooled and converted back to a liquid which was whisky. Of course, the near-by stream provided plenty of cool free water for cooling when the time came as well as water for mixing the mash in the barrels and for cleaning up in between times. Alva did not remember where he got the 'thumper' which is a somewhat special copper container that is in series with the piped steam from the pot and before the worm in the cooling barrel. In his still, he placed the thumper in it's own barrel. This was a common practice. The thumper helps remove some of the impurities on the first pass and therefore you are only required to run the distillation process once instead of two times. When the run is progressing as it should the 'Thumper' makes a slow hollow 'thump, thump' sound. Hence the name. He spliced all the pipes together with dough made from flour and water from the stream. The dough was cheap but there was a chemical reason for dough instead of solder. Aside from being quick and inexpensive, bread dough doesn't react to the alcohol going through the pipes like the lead based solder does. Alva did his last assembly of the pipes, the thumper, the cooling barrel which requires that creek water be piped to it in constant supply with the overflow from it spilling over and going back into the stream. When the mash is ready to 'run', a guy has to work fast to get the still parts out of hiding in the woods nearby and assemble it so that he can begin running the still. Alva said on this run and on many others he would arrive at the still before daylight with no light or any means of visibility except for moon light, hence the term 'Moonshine'. He would work all day and until it was too dark to see without stopping, without eating and without making unnecessary noise. When the day was done, he would have about 30 gallons of high proof moonshine whiskey. I've left out the task of keeping the wood fire burning properly so that the pot boiled but didn't blow up and cutting and making a fire from oak, really dry oak, so that it didn't smoke and give away his position in the woods. Also, all day as the pot would boil down to the bottom, he would move the fire to one side, leave it burning, tip the pot over on it's side, use creek gravel to wash and scrub it, use the cool creek water to rinse it, tip it back up and put it on the rock supports to level it again, fill it with fresh mash, use the still burning fire to rekindle fresh wood, really dry wood, he had gathered earlier, and get ready to catch the first of the distilled spirits. About a gallon or more of the first of the distillation must be discarded because it is poison. The first of the distillation process contains methanol alcohol. If the first of the run, which is high in methanol alcohol content, are consumed the drinker will get a headache or worse. Alva, or any good whisky maker, can determine this by tasting (not swallowing) the product until the proper mix is coming from the worm which is being cooled in the cooling barrel. Only the final tip of the worm protrudes from the bottom of the cooling barrel. Modern day makers use a hygrometer. Alva used no thermometer or instruments to test. He had a vast well of experience and a number of thumbnail tests taught to him by his brother, Charlie. The same is true at the end of the run along with a 'bump test' of alcohol content and tasting. Alva would put a small quantity in a pint bottle, turn the bottle on it's side, then slam the bottle against the palm of his other hand three times. When he stopped, he'd watch the size and quantity of the bubbles which he called 'frog eyes' float on the surface. The quality of those bubbles, the length of time they floated before breaking up, the quantity of them and their average diameter all added up to his test. He'd do this test three or four times to determine the whisky quality. The very last of the distillation process was discarded because it, too, contained toxins and a variety of unhealthy substances.

When it was right, he'd say, "Look at them frog eyes. That's good whisky."

As an aside to this: Years later when Alva aged and retired from any and all Moonshining, he would purchase a small bottle of whisky from a liquor store just for "sippin". Before he would make the purchase and regardless of the label of the whisky, he would instinctively slam the selected bottle into the palm of his hand three times and watch the 'bead'.

I've seen him return quality labeled, expensive whisky to the shelf with the comment, "That's no good. Let me check something else."

He would sometimes go through three or four bottles before he found one that 'beaded' to his satisfaction. Often the one selected was a lower priced whiskey than the one I had first offered for his inspection. It was not uncommon for the proprietor of store to question what he was doing.

Alva would answer, "I'm just checkin' to see if you have any good whisky in your store. I'm going to buy a bottle if I find one that's any good. I've made a lot of it, so I know how to test it. Most of what I've checked so far is not very good whisky."

The store operator would become interested and soon, after a short lesson by Alva, he would begin checking bottles himself. It was not unusual to observe such a scenario that lasted several minutes. Eventually, a bottle would be found that met Alva's criteria. The purchase would be made and we would continue on our way.

Alva would say upon leaving, "That guy seemed like he was interested in learning how to check his whisky. I'll bet he never knew how to check it before. Most people don't." After a pause, he'd concluded, "I didn't want to make him feel bad but, the truth was, none of his whisky was very good."

The last of the run is commonly called 'singlings'. It cannot be consumed either. All the whiskey that is judged consumable from the run, the middle portion, is mixed together and divided into containers. One gallon jugs work best for this initial dividing and mixing. Ultimately, 5 gallon jugs are used for long term storage and for transporting it. A five gallon jug in a tow sack is certainly a familiar sight. The odors of the whiskey and that of the damp tow sacks remind me of my dad. Anytime I catch a whiff of either of those I can picture my dad in his black felt hat working in the woods with the whisky. He'd take out his perpetual white handkerchief from his right rear pants pocket, wipe the sweat from his forehead and comment on how close he was to completion.

After I was big enough, I'd 'watch' for him. That 'watch' consisted of carrying a gun while standing a slight distance away from where he was measuring up gallon jugs.

Alva would say, "Go up on that little hill there." He would point to a particular nearby rise. He wanted to know exactly where I was going to stand watch. He would say, "Go up there and watch for me while I finish measuring up the run. I've got two more barrels to run and then I'm finished." Alva would caution me to stand still up on the rise. He would say, "Stand still and mostly listen. If you hear somebody, fire one shot straight up. I will know what it means and they, whoever they are, will be diverted over to you. When they arrive, tell them you shot a rabbit. Point the opposite direction from me and ask them to help you look for it. That will give me plenty of time to get away in the opposite direction.

As an afterthought, he'd say, "I'll be watching and listening to what is going on. If I don't hear anything to worry about, I'll catch up to you as you head for home. Follow the creek the still is on down stream and I'll find you pretty quick. I won't leave until we are joined up again."

He used a clever little siphon hose that he carried to do the 'measuring up'.. He would set the five gallon jug slightly higher than the one gallon jug. He'd stick the end of the siphon hose into the larger jug, suck on the loose end of the hose slightly and then stick the loose end into the gallon jug. Nearly as soon as he placed the end of the hose into the gallon jug, a stream of moonshine would begin flowing into it. This procedure was far easier than lifting the large jug full of liquid and pouring it into the gallon jug. Often if the ground was level and there was nothing to elevate the larger container Alva would sit the large container on his knee to give it the necessary height for a gravity flow. When he was doing this he was required to pay careful attention to the operation to avoid spilling the whisky or breaking a container. That's why he needed me to be his eyes during this period.

Sometimes, the gun I carried was my choice. It was either my 22 Winchester automatic rifle, a 12 gauge double barrel shotgun and/or our Colt 38 Super automatic pistol. In the later years, I carried the 38 Super and/or a Model 94 30-30 Winchester. Alva knew I was a good shot but he preferred I carry the shotgun.

His words were, "When you're excited or it's dusky dark a shotgun gets it done better than a rifle at close range." He would always finish by saying, "Now if anything happens, know where I am and don't shoot me." Then he would add, "I don't want you to shoot anybody unless you think he's going to kill one of us. I'll leave that decision up to you. It's best if no one ever gets killed, including us."

Well, he may have left the 'decision' up to me but I knew quite well that I'd better make that decision agree with him. I always did as he asked for hell was to pay if I didn't. Although I've strayed away from the original topic, whisky business was a composite of many things. Moonshining was such a blend of life's features and needs that it is difficult to separate it into specific categories. It's like trying to separate the hard breathing from the sweating on one of those hot Arkansas days. You just do both at once without segregating one from the other.

At the still, constant tasting is required to determine the exact time to cut off the run and dump the remaining mash before it becomes toxic. Although the quality of the whiskey is determined by the mix of the mash and time allowed for it to "work" before distillation begins, the drinkability of the final product is determined largely by how much of the whiskey is kept for consumption and how much is discarded at the beginning and the end of a run. Only the middle portion of the run is suitable for drinking. This is one of the two places where the real artistry of whiskey making dwells. The other is the mixing of the mash. Alva was a master at both stages of the process. Consequently, Alva's whiskey was always complimented highly as having the greatest flavor with the smoothest taste and without giving the drinker a headache or a hangover. Many of the professional people in Hot Springs who became his customers, included doctors, lawyers, judges and undertakers. Many had consumed whiskies from many sources including many illegal sources. Obviously, there were connoisseurs among those customers. All of whom I heard comment on it described it as the "best they had ever tasted and without after effects."

More than once I have heard the comment, " Mr. Burris, I hope you never decide to get out of this business. I'll buy all like this that you can make."

There would be a big laugh all around and Alva would thank them for their comments. He took their compliments seriously

CHAPTER NINE

Alva

Whisky Beginnings

Whisky making is not an eight hour a day job

I'm going to regress slightly to a period prior to my birth and prior to the events I just described to you and return to that period when Alva, Violet and the two girls had returned from California and relay what Alva described as his whisky beginnings.

Alva told me, "I first started to make a little whiskey and selling it after Violet and I got back to Arkansas from California. It was the first time in years that I had any money in my pocket. It was the first time that I was able to save some money over and above what I was spending for expenses for the family. It was the first time that I had felt good about supporting my family for several years."

He said, "I finally felt like I was doing my job."

He went on, "I saved enough that I leased a little land and began planting what I called a 'truck patch'. It was just a small garden of vegetables that I could easily grow and sell from the back of a truck. It mainly consisted of watermelons, cantaloupes, tomatoes, potatoes, corn, cucumbers and okra. It was healthy food that everyone likes to eat."

He planted about an acre in various vegetables. He worked it all himself by hand without power tools. He owned no farm equipment to speak of. Both he and Violet would pick when the items were ripe. Alva would take the truck, loaded with vegetables, to Hot Springs and sell all day. They would pick all one day and sell all the next day.

Alva said, "We worked hard but we had plenty to eat without buying it." He told me how he purchased a few pigs, which he kept in a pen. He fed the pigs all the left over vegetables and waste side of the garden. Soon he purchased a cow that provided all their milk. They sold some of the excess milk and butter also. Naturally, the cow got leftovers and waste from the garden. He fed both the cow and the pigs the waste from the fermented mash from the still after he strained it.

He said, "I had to be careful not to give them too much because it had a little alcohol in it. It seemed like it gave them an appetite. They loved it. Especially, the pigs. They gained a lot of weight because it gave them an appetite."

The manure from both the cows and pigs went back on the garden along with the chicken manure. They had purchased several chickens by now and those provided all the eggs they needed plus some to sell and occasionally one for Sunday dinner.

After picking the vegetables and loading the little truck, Alva would drive the truck down the street in the residential areas of Hot Springs and yell "Vegetables, vegetables". He said people would come out and buy all he had on board in a short time. He said sometimes he would run out of produce and promise to make another run the following day. He said they would be waiting on the curb for him when he pulled up without him saying a word. He enjoyed this. When he told me about it, with a smile on, I could see that he had enjoyed it tremendously.

Whiskey making is not an eight hour a day job. Although when you begin a run you may work hard and long hours from before daylight into the night, there are many days where you don't even go near the still site. Periodic visits must be made to barrels to test the mash to determine when it is properly fermented and ready to "run". Customers must be sought out during this dead time. Alva had clever ways to determine who might be a potential whiskey customer as he was selling vegetables. He was good at what we now refer to as social engineering. He could size up a person in a heartbeat and know what questions to ask.

He would ask questions such as, "I wonder where a person could buy a drink of good old moonshine whiskey".

He would never ask who wanted to buy from him. He took the high road. If he found where he could buy a drink, then he knew immediately where he could sell some, without asking directly. That avoided suspicion.

Between 'truck farming' and 'moonshining' Alva had found work, finally, in a big way. He was certainly not picking cotton at the rate of $1.50 per 100 pounds in California anymore. Sounds like he was working day and night. He likely was. He was saving money. He told me that the period I was just describing was one of the happiest times of his life. I believe it was. He was in perfect health. He had a young family and his girls, Leona and Margaret, were just beginning school. He was depositing money in the bank regularly.

CHAPTER TEN

Visit by the KKK

"We were just anxious to make friends and earn a living". Alva Burris

While Alva, Violet and the two girls, Leona and Margaret lived in the old house, made whisky and grew vegetables for sale, the word got out that he was living successfully. Word may have gotten around that he was making some whisky. Not all the neighbors were happy to see someone doing well in their midst. Times were still pretty tough for the average family. Anyone who seemed successful was under instant suspicion. Alva said to me that he never fully understood why some of the people developed a grudge against him. He said it could have been his success or it could have been that they detected his whisky business. He said he never knew the reason.

Regardless of the reason, some disliked him. There were subtle messages relayed to him that clearly said they didn't like him and his family. Alva paid no attention to the negative comments because they were greatly outweighed by the positive response from other neighbors. However, after a while he began to hear an additional note of disapproving comments. He heard, through a friend, that the Klu Klux Klan, the KKK, had become stronger in the area. He heard that the KKK was increasing it's membership and aggressively attempting to attract new members by committing violent acts against people they 'decided' were undesirable. The KKK was firmly against black citizens and anyone who fraternized with black people. At the time, black people were called Negros or worse. The 'African American' label had not been invented. 'Negro' was the polite name which black people preferred to be called. The KKK was firmly against 'Negro Lovers'. That title applied to anyone who did business with Negros, spoke to them at length, allowed them to come inside one's residence, or generally was civil to them. If your family shared a meal with a Negro family that was the worst of all offenses in the eyes of the KKK. That would surely bring the wrath of their Grand Wizard down upon you and likely down upon the Negro family as well. It could mean the death of the Negro family. Alva did plenty of business with the Negro community when he sold his vegetables. His whisky business was, at that time, equally divided between black and white customers with more of it going to white customers in the Hot Springs vicinity.

As Alva's vegetable business grew, he and his family were frequently invited to have dinner (that was the mid day meal in Arkansas. Supper was the evening meal) by one of his customers. Often the invitation was from a Black family.

Alva said, "Several times when Violet and the kids were with me, one of the families that I sold vegetables to would invite us to have dinner with them. They were all such nice people. We accepted many times and had fun talking to them. They were generous and humorous. Violet and the kids enjoyed it. It had not been that long since we had been in the farm labor camps in California. We were all anxious to have friends and customers of any flavor. We didn't care whether they were black or white. We were just anxious to make friends and earn a living. Sometimes, we invited one of the families to have a Sunday dinner with us. On those occasions we would kill a big hen and cook it. Violet was a good cook and she loved cooking for everyone."

Apparently, this behavior was eventually noticed by some of the KKK members. Alva suspected that they saw him 'fraternizing' with the Negro community.

Alva told me, "I hadn't made any enemies with anyone. We had mostly been working hard and keeping to our selves because we were so busy. We hadn't had time to make anyone mad."

Nevertheless, Alva and his family became aware of the boiling resentment among the few. While most of the neighbors acted OK, a few began refusing to speak to him or Violet when their paths crossed. Alva found this suspicious. He asked one of the neighbors what had changed to make them act differently.

Alva was told that the Klu Klux Klan was aggressively attempting to attract new members. The KKK was struggling to gain power in the vicinity. They needed someone with whom they could make an example. They wanted to make an example of someone who fraternized with Negro people. They had brought up his residence in the area at one of their secret masked, robed meetings. Alva was told that they were 'discussing what to do about his presence in their community'.

Alva was surprised but finally understood the change in attitude. He said to me, "I didn't change a thing I was doing because we were doing nothing wrong. I wasn't about to run from them just because they took a dislike to our friends."

Alva said, "Shortly after I learned this, a young man whom I knew, but not well, came to me one evening. He said he was a courier from the Klu Klux Klan. He said that he had been chosen to deliver a message to me from the Klan, the KKK.

He said the 'Klan' was going to pay me a visit. He said they were planning to 'burn me out' if we had not moved within a week after getting the message."

Alva said, "The courier gave me the date and the evening when the event was to occur. The messenger told me that we had been seen having dinner with a Negro family in Hot Springs more than once. Also, the Klan had seen a Negro family eating at our house more than once. He said the Klan had assigned an observer to watch me after noticing how many Negro friends we had. They watched us and decided that the Klan wanted us out of the neighborhood."

In 'Klan speak' that meant they would come, set the house on fire, no matter who was in it. They would set a wooden cross on the front yard and light the cross on fire for all to see that 'this family violated Klan rules'. Now, in many cases, the burning of the cross would be done first as a warning. The second step was 'burning the person out' which, interpreted, meant burning the resident's home with them in it if they didn't escape. In this instance, for whatever the reason, the Klan had decided to go straight to plan B and burn Alva and his family out on the first visit.

Alva told me this story more than once. He was concerned for himself and his family. He said, "I didn't know just what I was going to do. I did know that I wasn't going to run from this group. I knew that part for sure. I'd heard too much about their dirty ways already. I was afraid, but I was determined not to give in to them because they were an evil bunch. I wasn't going to give up the happiness Violet, the kids and I were experiencing to a bunch of Klu Klux Klansmen."

Alva said, "I told the courier, whom I knew casually, to come sit down because I had a message to send back in return. I told him I wanted his close attention so that he wouldn't forget a word I was about to say."

Alva said, "I didn't know exactly what I was going to say but I was forming the message as we walked to a place to sit. I was getting more and more angry as we walked. My plan was cemented into my mind by the time we sat down. I knew for damned sure my plan would not include running."

Alva said, "He was a young guy who probably didn't realize what he was getting into by joining up with the Klan. I told him to sit down beside me and pay close attention. I said to him, I don't know the name of the person who sent you and I don't need to know who it is. I want you to listen very carefully and deliver this message exactly as I say it, to whomever sent you here. No intermediaries. I want you to tell that person and the group he represents, that you delivered the message and that I understood the message. Tell him I accept the message. Tell him that on that night that they plan to visit me and 'burn me out', I will be here as they expect me to be. Tell them to come ahead as they have planned. I will be expecting them to keep their word and fulfill their promise to me by showing up. Also, tell them this: Tell them that I said all of them should kiss their wives and children goodbye before they leave on the journey because many of them will not be returning home again. Be sure to tell them the whole thing. Don't leave a damn word of it out."

Alva told me that the courier looked surprised and scared. He said the eyes of the courier were big and he said he couldn't believe I was choosing to stand up against the Klan. However, he listened and promised to deliver the message, verbatim.

Alva said, "I waited on the designated night. I waited with gun loaded and plenty of ammunition. At that time I owned a nice 30-30 caliber Winchester model 94 with lever action. I fully expected them to arrive and attempt to burn my house. I had already moved Violet and the kids out of the house earlier in the day just in case they did show up. I took Violet and the kids over to her folk's house earlier but I left a lamp burning in the house so they would think someone was home. No one was there but me. I waited. Nobody showed up. I wasn't in the main house. I was waiting in a little shed nearby. The shed had a back door that would let me escape if necessary. I had planned to shoot the first guy who lit a torch before he could throw it on the house. I'd planned to get as many of the others as possible from where I was hiding before they could do anything. I was a good shot and the gun was nearly new. I was very confident that I could hold them off. I never got my chance. No one showed up."

Alva said, "Later, I asked around through different channels as to what happened on that night. The story was they decided, after hearing the courier's return message that the risk was too high. They abandoned any 'discipline' that they felt I deserved. I believe they made a wise decision."

The KKK was a mean and vindictive group that increased in popularity during that period right after the depression. They still exist, today, but have much less influence than they did then. Now, they mostly exist in name only with only small pockets that maintain the original theme of hatred.

CHAPTER ELEVEN

Whisky in Virginia

The sale of anything without first jumping through the proper legal hoops and paying taxes, constitutes the term 'Bootlegger'.

Whisky production deserves some history so that you can understand the origin of the liquid I am discussing. Law abiding, God fearing people made and drank whisky before they crossed the Atlantic to form the colonies. Government pounced on the concept of 'taxing' the substance almost from the beginning. The taxing has been refined, omitted for brief periods, reinstated when money was needed to help pay for wars and mostly increased for the benefit of those who collected it. The tax was never intended to be a deterrent for the consumption of whisky. Tax has always been a revenue machine. It remains as such today.

The process of manufacturing whisky deserves that we go back and examine some history to properly understand how all this

Moonshining came into existence. The 'process' that Alva perfected for himself deserves a bit of examination to understand what had to be performed in order to produce drinkable spirits.

Most agree that whisky making in the United States originated on the east coast and spread quickly west as the population did. Virginia whisky making had some deep roots. Here are some fundamentals of the process.

The difference between a legal distiller and a moonshiner is basic: The moonshiner chooses not to license his distilling operation or pay taxes on the whiskey he produces. The British and Scottish began taxing whiskey in the mid-1600s, and by 1700 the British were calling brandy smugglers on the coast of England 'moonlighters'. Later, in the Virginia Blue Ridge Mountains, the illegal distiller came to be called a 'moonshiner' or a 'bootlegger'. The term, *Moonshiner* actually refers to the manufacture of spirits while *Bootlegger* refers to the illegal sale of it or any controlled item whereby the seller circumvents the tax. For instance: You could be labeled a 'bootlegger' if you sold tobacco without paying the proper taxes. The sale of anything without first jumping through the proper legal hoops and paying taxes, constitutes the term 'Bootlegger'.

In the early 1900s Roanoke, Virginia, was a young rapidly growing city, and the Casper Company was one of several legal alcohol producers serving the area.

The United States collected an excise tax on alcohol from 1791 to 1802. There was a gap in the collection and then again from 1813 to 1817. Alcohol went untaxed for the next 45 years, but in the midst of the Civil War, Congress again passed a whiskey tax. They needed the revenue. By 1865 the tax was two dollars per gallon, up to 12 times the actual cost of making a gallon of liquor.

THIS IS AN EARLY JUG FROM THE ROANOKE VIRGINIA AREA

Though some people avoided taxes by running illegal stills, by the 1880's dozens of Blue Ridge distillers were operating under state licenses. With improved roads and railroads, alcohol could be shipped easily from the Blue Ridge to coal camps, factory towns, and larger cities. In 1893-94 Franklin County, Virginia, alone, had 77 legal distilleries. Most of these were producing brandy from apples or peaches under three-month licenses after the fruit harvest.

THIS IS A TYPICAL LABEL FROM A CONTAINER OF THAT ERA

Numerous Virginia Blue Ridge distilleries, such as Patrick County's F. DeHart Distillery, operated under legal licenses in the late 1800s and early 1900s.

As the 1800's drew to a close, the national stance against alcohol was gaining ground. Around the turn of the century, laws were passed making it illegal to run a distillery in a rural area, and through the early 1900s, one by one, Virginia counties banned the sale and production of alcohol. The churches pushed a lot of these laws through. When North Carolina outlawed the making (though not the selling) of whiskey, some Carolina distilleries moved into Virginia. By 1909 most of Virginia and about half of the Blue Ridge was "dry." Licensed distilleries were forced to close. In 1914 the Commonwealth voted to ban alcohol statewide. (The Blue Ridge county of Franklin consistently voted against the ban.) Prohibition was enforced nationwide in 1920, and not surprisingly in hindsight, the market for moonshine, which had been growing steadily over the years, exploded as I mentioned earlier.

Money, of course, has always driven the moonshining industry. Over the past century some people made fortunes in the trade. The big earners were the men providing the operating money and supplies for large operations. In the southern Virginia Blue Ridge local history tells of a few such bootleggers having tens of thousands of dollars in cash in the midst of the Great Depression of the 1930s. One wealthy Franklin County moonshiner bought an airplane so his son could fly over and see if their still sites were well hidden from the air.

CHAPTER TWELVE

Arkansas Prohibition

Candidates typically won favor with voters by providing ample amounts of whiskey on Election Day.

Making and selling whisky in Arkansas or the area that would become Arkansas has a history going back to as early as 1760. Arkansas has been a state since 1836. Before statehood when Arkansas was in its territorial period, the authorities attempted to limit use of alcoholic beverages through legal efforts such as establishing 'dry' counties, as well as through extra-legal measures such as destroying whiskey distilleries. Since achieving statehood in 1836, prohibition has consistently been a political and public health issue in Arkansas.

As early as the 1760's, European settlers at Arkansas Post, which is now Arkansas County, took steps to limit alcohol use by Quapaw Indians living in the area. When the area in Arkansas was under Spanish control, British traders successfully maneuvered to trade goods and spirits in Arkansas, plying the Quapaw with rum despite a Spanish law prohibiting the providing of alcohol to natives. The Spanish, in turn, often used alcohol as a diplomatic tool for settling disputes with Indians. By the early 1780s, Spanish-controlled Arkansas settled on heavily regulating the production and sale of alcohol, falling just short of outright prohibition. As early as that, the use and sale of alcohol was a paradox of rules and abuse as it would continue to exist right up into my lifetime.

Control of alcohol initially focused on consumption by Native Americans, but as Arkansas's population began to increase, interest in prohibition began to widen. Most resistance was initiated by the churches. In the early nineteenth century, as Indians began resettling in present-day Oklahoma in accordance with the Indian Removal Act of 1830, a commander at nearby Ft. Smith, Lieutenant Gabriel Rains, organized a sting operation to disrupt the widespread illegal alcohol trade with Indians. The operation had limited success.

In 1832, a grand jury was empanelled to assess the problem of alcohol in Arkansas Territory which would be known as Arkansas. The jury attempted to invoke an outdated Spanish law that prohibited alcohol production and sale, but it could not enforce the ordinance. The emerging Arkansas middle class grew alarmed by the frequent, alcohol-fueled unrest that seemed to surround taverns. There was also a developing sense that alcohol hindered the ability of workers and craftsman to perform their jobs adequately, which some business owners feared would result in lower profits. The rising resistance to alcohol use coincided with the sweeping antebellum religious revival known as the Second Great Awakening. This was a national temperance movement that emerged in the 1820s and quickly spread to the drink-sodden South. In Arkansas, drinking was not only an everyday fact of life but also an integral part of state politics, since candidates typically won favor with voters by providing ample amounts of whiskey on Election Day.

The organized temperance movement in Arkansas began in earnest with the formation in 1831 of the Little Rock Temperance Society, which was closely aligned with local churches. Methodists were usually the most ardent in supporting prohibition, while Baptists were not widely involved in opposing alcohol until after the Civil War. At first, Arkansas temperance advocates spoke against whiskey and other 'hard' liquors while tacitly condoning beer and wine consumption. Significantly, the Little Rock Temperance Society, unlike other such organizations, allowed women to join its ranks. This opened the door for greater female participation in state politics. Women eventually formed the heart of the prohibition movement in Arkansas, opposing alcohol as a threat to the family structure. In the final assessment of the next Temperance Movement, more damage to home life had been done by the Movement than by the drinking of the spirits.

In the more rustic parts of the state, alcohol consumption was essentially immune to efforts to curb its abuse. Nevertheless, William Woodruff, founder and publisher of the Arkansas Gazette, a newspaper, cosponsored an 1841 rally to encourage the state legislature to outlaw liquor sales. In the 1850s, the Arkansas General Assembly moved to ban the manufacture and sale of alcohol, but this measure did little to curtail consumption. You can't stop people from drinking alcohol when they want it. Thus, while alcohol use thrived during the decade, so too did efforts to ban or limit its sale. For instance, in 1854, saloons and stills throughout Hempstead County were boarded up and closed by order of local officials. An 1855 law gave municipalities the power to ban alcohol, mandating that prospective taverns be approved by a local majority. This established a precedent that largely still exists today, as counties have been able to hold referendums on whether or not to allow alcohol to be sold within their borders. This was the beginning of the Wet County -- Dry County choice in Arkansas. That choice still exists.

The push for prohibition generally came from emerging urban centers such as Little Rock, where residents worried that the state's economic development would be hampered by Arkansas's reputation as an intemperate frontier. Some of the state's most notorious outposts known for libertine attitudes toward drink, such as Napoleon, now named Desha County, were subject to attacks from temperance advocates.

The Civil War brought greater efforts by state leaders to prohibit the sale of liquor. In 1862, under Confederate rule, the state government passed a statewide ban on distilleries in order to save grain for the war effort. This did little to curb backwoods 'bootleg' whiskey production, and indeed, many prominent Arkansans openly ignored the law, such as Fayetteville County judge David Walker, who proclaimed that he would pay "any price in or out of reason" to acquire whiskey. In 1864, the state's efforts to stop the production of alcohol fell apart when the Governor signed a bill that allowed distilleries to pay the state for the right to produce alcohol. After the war, amid renewed calls for temperance, the Republican Party embraced the issue as part of a broader platform that endorsed greater government activism on social causes. In an attempt to limit election fraud, Arkansas Republicans passed legislation banning the sale of alcohol on Election Day, while making it illegal to refuse to sell alcohol on the basis of race. In many towns, African Americans, known at the time as Negros, were regularly denied alcohol for fear of social unrest. At the time, Indians and Negroes were widely believed to be unable to control themselves after consuming alcohol.

In the post-war era, farmers found they could earn far greater profits by growing corn for the production of alcohol than by growing corn or other agricultural products for direct human consumption. The spread of moonshine stills and the illegal trade in alcohol spurred response from Arkansas law enforcement. Throughout the 1870s, in what became known as the "moonshine wars," federal revenue agents (who assailed moonshine as a violation of the law because it was being sold without paying the requisite liquor tax. Notice: revenue/money was the key word here) fanned out across the hilly terrain of northern Arkansas in search of illegal stills. Raids against moonshiners, also known as 'wildcatters', were common, and stories of violent shootouts were vividly recounted in local newspapers. Local officials often sided with wildcatters in opposition to federal authorities, and jury nullification, in which accused wildcatters were given extremely light sentences or acquitted, was commonplace. In the 1890s, John Burris, a deputy revenue collector, personally closed over 150 stills and investigated hundreds more while posing as a timber buyer. Alva told me the story of John Burris. As far as he knew, Alva said he knew of no direct relationship of John Burris to our Burris strain.

Meanwhile, in communities throughout Arkansas, women were increasingly engaged in urging saloons to close. These were characteristically women heavily involved in church activities. Local chapters of the Woman's Christian Temperance Union, WCTC, the leading national organization for alcohol reform, sprang up across the state. By the late 1880s, over 100 anti-saloon or temperance organizations existed in the state, seeking not only legislative reform but also encouraging young Arkansans to pledge to "abstain from intoxicating liquors." The efforts of temperance proponents culminated in substantial policy of reform. In 1871, the General Assembly voted to allow local referendum to decide whether saloons should be banned within three miles of colleges and schools. Eight years later, the legislature passed a law that called for towns to hold referendums every two years on whether or not to allow the sale of alcohol in quantities less than five gallons. This caused many saloons and stills to go out of business and resulted in gradual, piecemeal prohibition.

The prohibition movement gained momentum in the first decade of the twentieth century as Arkansas, and indeed much of the nation, continued to ban saloons. In 1906, sixty percent of American towns had done so, and the Arkansas chapter of the Anti Saloon League, founded in 1899, urged for more restrictions. In this period, Arkansas governors such as George Donaghey led the way for tighter control of alcohol.

Race played a role in local referendums as in 1913, when the legislature passed a bill that required petitions in support of a new saloon to be signed by a majority of white voters. In an era of widespread African-American voter disfranchisement, black opinion on alcohol was simply ignored or suppressed. By 1914, only nine Arkansas counties had managed to keep their saloons open. In 1915, the General Assembly passed the Newberry Act, effectively banning the manufacture and sale of alcohol in the state. In addition, the act failed to exempt the sale of alcohol for medicinal purposes.

In 1916, 'wets', or those who favored loosening alcohol restrictions, managed to campaign successfully for a referendum on the issue, but efforts to repeal the Newberry Act and restore liquor sales failed by a two-to-one margin. Prohibitionists prevailed, in part because they appealed to prominent African Americans such as Scipio Jones, who urged black Arkansans who were able to vote to support a ban on alcohol. The following year, the legislature made Arkansas one of the first states to pass complete prohibition by outlawing the importation of alcohol. Governor Charles Brough always a proponent of prohibition, signed the bill at the state Chamber of Commerce. When the United States entered WW1 in 1917, the national move toward prohibition gained the final motivation it needed, as the war effort's demand for grain, a key ingredient for producing liquor, outweighed the need for alcohol. As such, Congress passed the Eighteenth Amendment, Prohibition, which Arkansas ratified in January 1919.

During the 1920s, the temperance movement formed an unlikely partnership with the resurgent Ku Klux Klan or KKK, which claimed to have over 50,000 members in Arkansas at its peak. The membership was likely much higher than the figure given. For instance, Lula Markwell, former president of the Arkansas chapter of the WCTU, was the Imperial Commander of the Women of the Ku Klux Klan. The Klan was particularly active in the oil boomtowns of southern Arkansas, such as those in Union County, where bootleggers and gamblers openly flouted laws prohibiting the use and sale of whisky. In November 1922, a group of KKK calling themselves the "Cleanup Committee" launched attacks on liquor and gambling dens, expelling an estimated 2,000 people from the town of Smackover in Union County. By the late 1920s, the assault on liquor was subsequently taken up by Homer Atkins, sheriff of

Pulaski County and later governor of Arkansas. Of course, the KKK was more notorious as a white supremacist group who violently opposed increased Negro influence and affluence.

Joseph Robinson, longtime Democratic senator from Arkansas, was never a supporter of Prohibition, and he used the sweeping victory in the 1932 elections as an opportunity to draft legislation ending Prohibition. The onset of the Great Depression had encouraged many Americans to view repealing the ban on alcohol as economically beneficial. Indeed, by the early 1930s, the public's mood toward alcohol had softened. With the repeal of the Eighteenth Amendment in 1933, the entire state of Arkansas was once again wet. This ushered in a new phase in the state's history of alcohol control, in which prohibition was determined county by county. A 1935 state law mandated that, in order to hold a referendum on the matter, a petition had to be signed by at least thirty-five percent of a county's electorate. This was a formidable hurdle to "dry" advocates, and throughout the 1930s, liquor flowed relatively freely throughout the state.

While the national prohibition movement collapsed following World War II, Arkansas temperance advocates still pushed for dry counties but also had to reconcile with Arkansans' changing attitudes toward consumption. The business community, once stalwart dry proponents, no longer sided with the fading temperance movement. Indeed, from the late 1940's through the 1960's, the Dries suffered one setback after another. Winthrop Rockefeller, governor of the state during the late 1960s, argued that liquor sales would boost tourism and stimulate the economy.

Efforts to prohibit the sale and consumption of alcohol have existed throughout Arkansas's history, from before the territorial era to the present day. The peak of the state's prohibition movement, roughly from the 1850s through the 1920s, witnessed a confluence of disparate political forces all aiming to curb the use and abuse of alcohol. Prohibitionists came in several forms, from health and anticrime advocates to religious leaders, business owners, women, and even white supremacists. Though each of these groups came to support prohibition for their own personalized reasons, usually money, they found common ground and on their surface claimed that alcohol represented a scourge and a threat to the state of Arkansas. Many Arkansans believed the groups were largely hypocritical in their actions. Often the most outspoken prohibitionist were avid consumers of alcohol. The state law makers often professed to be on the side of the prohibitionists while welcoming the tax derived from the sale of whisky. For the uneducated, the production of untaxed whisky, or Moonshine, was an alternate method to earn money.

CHAPTER THIRTEEN

Making the Whisky

"As far as I know, no one has ever gotten sick on whiskey that I made." Alva Burris

Today a gallon of moonshine costs just over half the retail price of a gallon of the cheapest legal whiskey sold in liquor stores. Obviously there is still money to be made in dodging the tax. Here's how whisky is made:

Subject: "PREPAREDNESS"

The whole nation is talking "PREPAREDNESS," so why not the individual PREPARE? Prepare for the coming prohibition drouth that hits Virginia on November 1st, this year, 1916

On and after that date you will not have the privilege of fortifying your home with pure 100 proof Mountain Rose Corn Whiskey, made and sold strictly on its merits; nothing purer or better for medicinal purposes, regardless of the price you pay.

Good Whiskey will be Hard to Procure

at any price after our state goes dry, and if procured it will cost you three to five times the price I charge you. It will be no bad idea to lay away a ten years' supply of CORN WHISKEY strictly for medicinal purposes, and you will never regret it. Do not fail to include in your purchase ample supply for the coming Xmas holidays, as it is going to be hard on a supposed free people to conform abruptly to the fake prohibition measures. You had better

"Make Hay While the Sun Shines"

Now, in conclusion will say, get your orders in early and avoid the rush that will prevail during the last days of October. Remember that all orders to be delivered in Virginia will have to be placed in due time to be filled and delivered to you on or before October 31st.

Thanking my many friends and customers for their past patronage, and hoping to be of further service in the last days of my present business career, I remain, Yours truly,

J. H. de-HART,

PROPRIETOR OF

THE MOUNTAIN ROSE DISTILLERY

PHILPOTT, VIRGINIA.

WHISKY INGREDIENTS:

Sugar
10 lbs. Whole kernel corn, untreated (it works quicker if you use chops or corn meal instead of whole kernel corn)
5 Gallons Water
1 Cup Yeast, champagne yeast starter

DIRECTIONS:

Put corn in a burlap bag and wet with warm water. Place bag in a warm dark
place and keep moist for about ten days. When the sprouts are about a 1/4" long
the corn is ready for the next step. Wash the corn in a tub of water, rubbing
the sprouts and roots off. If you are using chops, there will be no sprouts to rub off. Another advantage of using chops. Chops

can be purchased at animal feed stores. If you have sprouts, throw the sprouts and roots away and transfer the corn into your primary fermenter. With a pole or another hard object mash the corn. Here's another reason to use chops. No mashing of the kernels needed. Make sure all the kernels are cracked if using whole kernels. Next add 5 gallons of boiling water. When the mash cools add yeast. Seal fermenter and vent with a water sealed vent. Fermentation will take 7-10 days. After the fermentation seems to be done, add more yeast and sugar. This raises the alcohol content. Alva knew just when to do this. The timing is very important. When fermentation is finally done, pour into still by filtering through a thin pillow case (or cheese cloth) to remove all solids. If solids are allowed to go into the pot they will burn and give the whisky a bad flavor. Light up your fire and you are ready to start distilling some whisky.

The alcohol from a first 'run' through the still is a rough-tasting product called 'singlings'. Some make a second run of the singlings to mellow the taste. Alva never made a second run of the singlings. He used a thumper on the first run and discarded the beginning and end of each run to avoid the toxic ingredients. He told of how some makers used everything they distilled in an effort to make more money. Alva had more interest in the quality product that was safe to drink.

The moonshiner then "proofs" his whiskey, mixing weak and strong liquor to get the desired strength. The first of the run is the strongest with alcohol while the last of the run is the lowest in alcohol content. When the run was all equalized, Alva would add a small portion of water to each container to get the alcohol content just the way he wanted it. It was just over 100 proof when it was ready to sell. To remove any impurities, the whiskey is sometimes poured through hardwood ashes or a felt filter. I never remember Alva filtering whiskey in this fashion. I can remember him straining whisky through a cloth so that he could filter out trash such as bit of leaf or such. He was old school and had his way of doing things that worked for him. Alva also always dumped the singlings. He discarded the first of the run and the last of the run. He was determined to keep his whiskey good and never allow it to be contaminated with poisons.

I can remember Alva saying many times, "Most of these whiskey makers try to make too much money from it and that's why they sell people the parts of the whiskey that is no good. Some of them even add stuff to the whisky to make it bead better. People get sick and it gives the whole trade a bad name. I'd rather make a little less money and produce a high quality whiskey that will never make anyone sick."

He would finish by saying, "As far as I know, no one has ever gotten sick on whiskey that I made." He'd laugh a little and continue, "Of course, a few of them drank a little too much. They liked it and didn't know when to stop."

CHAPTER FOURTEEN

The Steam Still

Washing whisky jugs in the creek was kind of a family project.

Though never as common as the turnip and submarine stills, (those names relate to the shape of the apparatus not the use of turnips and submarines) the steam still has also been used by many moonshiners. The turnip style is the one chosen by illustrators to exemplify the moonshine whisky business. The turnip style is the type I never saw in use. Steam stills come in varying designs, but the idea is the same in each. A boiler containing water is heated, and the resulting steam is either released directly into fermented mash or is piped through the mash. The mash boils, and the alcohol vapors pass into a water-cooled worm (or a thumper keg and then a worm).

One important advantage of a steam outfit is that the mash never scorches. The flame is under the water boiler, not the pot containing the mash, and the temperature of the steam is constant. Stirring the mash is unnecessary. Steam stills also work much faster than the other still types.

In Alva's stills he boiled the mash directly in the pot. His was an exercise in simplicity when possible. He watched the pot carefully so that no solids were burned on the bottom of the pot. He also dumped the pot before it had cooked to the bottom. He avoided many pitfalls by dumping the first of the distilled spirits and by dumping the pot early.

In the 1970's the blackpot tradition took over moonshining. It was easier to construct. The bootlegger saw that the big money was in producing sugar liquor, alcohol made by repeatedly adding pure sugar to leftover mash. Blackpot sites often had several submarine pots going at once, some filled with fermenting sugar and mash, others being heated. Revenuers had begun using airplanes to spot still sites in the 1950's, but having switched to oil or propane burners, the bootlegger could set up his operation under roof or even underground. In 1993 Pittsylvania County agents found Virginia's largest blackpot site--thirty six 800 gallon black pot stills--inside a building.

According to old-timers today, the *quality* of liquor was abandoned for *quantity* with the introduction of blackpot distilling techniques. Alva stuck with the old school technique of quality first at the expense of some waste. The bootlegger's current market, however, is no longer the southern factory town, and contemporary moonshine customers apparently do not care too much about taste. On the East coast, today's blackpot sugar liquor goes to low-income neighborhoods in large urban areas such as Tidewater Virginia, Philadelphia, New York, and the District of Columbia.

Big Black Pot Still Site in Virginia. One of the largest ever captured.

LIQUOR CARS AND LIQUOR HAULER

Stacked nearly flush with the truck bed, the half load of liquor pictured here weighed over a 1,000 pounds, even in light plastic jugs. This particular load was captured in Franklin County, Virginia, 1979. Plastic jugs became common later after Alva had gotten completely out of the business. Alva always used glass jugs. He would have never considered plastic.

Alva used glass one-gallon jugs that he purchased from a soft drink bottling company in Hot Springs, Arkansas. I was along on most of the purchases to help with carrying the jugs, four to a cardboard box, out to the car. Alva, when asked what he was using them for, would answer that he was bottling spring water from Hot Springs and taking it home for later use. The employees who were gathering the empties from the bottling plant would cock their heads to one side, nod slowly and purse their lips forward in faux pout. That answer seemed to satisfy them. At least they didn't pursue the subject beyond his explanation.

We would haul those jugs home and wash the syrup out of them. They had labels which we would wash off. Alva didn't want anyone to trace the origin of the containers. At this stage I was considered too little to carry the jugs. I might break one. My Mom would take two at a time out to the creek behind our house and soak the labels off in the stream. Using just her nails, and sand from the creek bed, she would scrape them until they were clean. If any of the soft drink syrup was hardened and difficult to remove from the jug, she would get sand and gravel from the creek bottom and put a small amount in the jug. After putting a spin on the water and sand in the jug for a bit she would dump it out and wash it with some water from the creek. She'd hold it up to the light and smile.

She'd say, "Well, I got one more clean for your Daddy." Sometimes Alva came out with several in his hands. He often helped wash them too. Washing whisky jugs in the creek was kind of a family project.

When we were finished, Alva would put four in each gunny sack until they were all sacked. Then he would carry four sacks at a time up the trail into the woods where he hid them for his use at the still. My Mom would usually carry a sack of four over her shoulder while Alva carried 20. I would tag along behind with my mother nagging me to keep up. The trip to the area near the still was long. She was handy with the reminders of how many wild animals were in the woods and what would happen to me if I didn't keep up with her. I took the threats seriously but often interesting things along the trail would cause me to fall behind. My pockets were usually full of woodsy treasures by the time we reached our destination.

Songs were made of the trade. Here's the words to one I remember. It's not a very good song but it reflected what was happening.

Well I was going down Route 40 in a '57 Chevrolet,
Had a '59 Cadillac mill.
I had been up in the mountains hauling illegal whiskey
from a pure copper moonshine still.

FIRST VERSE OF THE SONG "GOING DOWN ROUTE 40," BY GARY THOMPSON

As immortalized in the film "Thunder Road," revenue agents have long gone after moonshine as it is being transported to market. Historically, the trip from still to buyer was uneventful in most cases. Yet if agents had a tip as to when and where a load of whiskey was being moved, revenuers might set up a roadblock or simply wait along the route for the 'hauler' or 'runner' to pass by.

DOUBLE SPRINGS ON THIS AXLE

Suspension enhancements, such as the extra leaf springs shown here on a 1951 Ford pickup truck, held vehicles level even when carrying a full load of whiskey. This particular truck was used to haul moonshine.

In the era prior to police two-way radios, a hauler could possibly outrun officers with a fast vehicle. Some of the resulting chases are the stuff of legend. Officers at times did shoot at the tires of their prey, and revenuers and liquor haulers alike suffered car crashes. If the hauler was spotted, he might lose his pursuer on dark country roads. Some skilled drivers perfected the "bootleg turn," a technique of spinning 180 degrees in a quick skid. With the flick of a special switch, a hauler could turn off his taillights, and occasionally vehicles were fitted with bright rear-facing lights to blind pursuing revenuers. If the hauler could not shake the agents, he might jump out of the car and run on foot into the woods, avoiding arrest but losing both the vehicle and the liquor. Years later, when I was older and driving, I learned the 180 early. I also practiced the 180 reverse turn where I would back up fast and spin the car around, shift from reverse to first during the spin by putting the transmission into second gear and then very quickly pulling the shift lever into first gear. During the turn it was neutral, second gear and quickly in to first, bury the throttle, let out the clutch and away you go. It takes a couple of tries to learn it. If it is done quickly, it works without the need for a fully synchronized transmission. When you see this done now in the movies, they are using an automatic transmission. It's extremely easy with an automatic. However, a three speed on the column without the benefit of a synchronized first gear is another animal. I wasted a couple of transmissions before I perfected it. Alva didn't complain much about those lost transmissions because the end result served his purposes.

Long before my introduction into the business as a hauler, haulers had no desire to draw attention to themselves by speeding or driving a conspicuous vehicle. Most runs were made at civilized speeds. Special springs and shocks were installed on cars and trucks to hold the vehicles level when loaded. The primary desire was to blend in and remain inconspicuous. At times drivers switched license plates to avoid identification.

Packed with up to 130 gallons of whiskey, the 1940 Ford coupe was the 'runner's' vehicle of choice well into the 1950's. Since the 1970's, haulers have switched to vans or pickup trucks with camper shells. Alva and I made many runs in a 1950 four door two toned green Chevrolet. My personal car was a 1951 Chevrolet with an Oldsmobile V8 engine equipped with three two barrel carbs and a 1937 Cadillac LaSalle transmission. I drove this same vehicle to high school daily.

Later, Alva purchased a one year old 1954 Chevrolet. It was maroon and white. We used it for a long time as our family car. It was also used to deliver a gallon to a customer from time to time. Each of our cars was well known to the local police. Often when we were driving and not hauling the police would pull us over and ask (demand) to search the vehicle. No search warrant was required then. All the doors and the trunk were opened. Any contents of any bags in the car were emptied and inspected. This search was always conducted with no warrant and usually on the side of the road. Sometimes it happened in town. I was always embarrassed. I was afraid that one of my friends would see us on the roadside with the police searching our car. The search usually took about 20 minutes. Once while we were stopped, Alva asked the sheriff who was conducting the search why they continued to harass us if they never found anything.

The sheriff looked knowingly at Alva and said, "Mr. Burris, if you would just see it in your heart to pay us what we have asked then we could prevent all this from happening. We have made it clear what we want. You continue to ignore our requests. We are trying to be nice to you."

Alva said, "To Hell with you. I'm not paying you anything. You're more dishonest than someone that sells whisky. You've tried to catch me doing it. You've stopped me 33 times in the past year. I've counted it. Never have you found a single thing for which to arrest me. Either you are a sorry excuse for what you do or I'm innocent and you are harassing me. Either way, you have nothing to prove the legitimacy of your searches. I'm tired of it and you can never scare me into paying you a damn cent."

The sheriff said, "Well, I've told you how you can stop all this and you won't abide by what I told you. It's going to go on and on until you finally see it our way."

Alva would end the conversation with his last word as the sheriff walked slowly back to his car and the others assisting him got into their cars. Alva would say, "You're never gettin' a damn dime from me this way. So give it up."

They never gave it up. Our cars were easily recognized. Alva got the idea that since our cars were easily recognized, we could go to a car lot, pretend to be interested in a used car, take the car for a test drive and deliver whisky to a customer during midday. That's what we did many times. I think he liked the challenge of it. I did.

My first time to drive a 1955 Chevrolet was on one of these runs. During another instance we 'borrowed' a 1957 Pontiac. The Pontiac was red and white. It was a four door hardtop. I think I fell in love with that car. I've liked them since that wild run. For my inexperienced foot, it was the fastest car I'd ever driven. Alva was in a different mode than he was normally. He seemed to depend on me. That, along with the opportunity to drive a car that I admired, fast, was a unique experience. During those runs were times when I felt equal to Alva. That was a unique and welcome feeling. As illegal as what we were doing was, I enjoy remembering those stolen minutes.

There were other 'borrowed' cars. A couple other 1955 Chevrolets, a 1955 Ford, an Oldsmobile that was 1955 or 1956. I've forgotten. They were very similar. The first time behind the wheel of that Pontiac was special, however.

CHAPTER FIFTEEN

Haulin'

Quick acquisition of a dirt road increased my chances of escape.

Much has been made in popular culture of the connection between liquor haulers and NASCAR auto racing, but in truth few moonshine drivers dabbled in organized racing. The real ties between the two activities took place in local garages where mechanics modified engines for speed and suspensions for handling. The mechanic's skills were useful to both stock car racers and moonshine runners. As for fancy driving, that was avoided unless one had to escape a trap. In all other cases, one was required to drive sensible and safe and avoid anything that made you appear different than the other drivers. I practiced matching the speed of other drivers and never passed illegally. Only if an attempt was made to stop me did I go into the race mode. Then, all bets were off. I drove to escape. That usually meant that I drove hard on the paved road and looked for a dirt road to switch to. Quick acquisition of a dirt road increased my chances of escape. I drove hard on the dirt road. Lots of dust was created. Dust was good cover. Then back onto pavement shortly before getting onto dirt again. I'd make it to my destination, unload the quantity that I carried and quickly get back on the road again. One of my jobs as a driver was to avoid telegraphing my destination. Good advance planning worked miracles. Sometimes a dry run was made first to shake out any suspicious vehicles. My runs were all made at night. My vehicle was much harder to identify in the darkness. My lights were shut off on the rear and I never allowed a police car or any car for that matter to get close enough to read the license. I knew all the back roads. It was very exciting. Although the most successful delivery was one in which no action took place, I yearned for the race. Each successful delivery that required high speed made me feel invincible. I did, for a teenager, become quite talented on the back roads. Now, with the benefit of age and multiple sanctioned races under my belt, I realize how naive I was during those years. I would complete my run and return to my house the back way, park in the yard alongside the house and go in the back door. I would turn on no lights and just sit in the front room and watch. I would sit there and watch the road. Once after one of those capers, I saw the sheriff drive by slowly and pause at the driveway. I was scared to death that he was going to come in. I guess he was satisfied with whatever he saw. He certainly didn't know I had just delivered whisky. Either way, he continued on down the road without coming into my house. I was never stopped while transporting although I was stopped and searched many times when no alcohol was on board. The cops would look at that Oldsmobile engine with three carburetors in that little Chevy and just shake their heads.

Alva was constantly afraid that the cops would plant some alcohol on the vehicle and then arrest me for transporting. That never happened. It was a valid worry.

I'm getting ahead of myself again so lets back up to Alva and Violet and that period before I existed.

Alva lead a productive and busy life as he farmed and made whiskey and garnered customers for each. Leona and Margaret grew up and found husbands. During that period, something happened between Alva and Violet. A deep emotional riff developed between them. I was never sure of the exact reason for it but only that he told me that he promised Violet during that period when he was working and farming and making whisky that when the girls left home, he would divorce her. Alva took the reason for that decision to his grave. The last girl to leave home was Margaret. He told me, with obvious pride, that the day Margaret left home he announced to Violet that he too was leaving as he had promised years earlier. I am baffled by the riff that developed between them. Years later I experienced them together again and he seemed to care a great deal for her. His care for her was obvious. Equally obvious to me was the love she seemed to have for him. Their separation baffled me. Each continued life and married someone else. Violet had no additional children. Something strange happened which culminated in his departure.

Alva and Grant with the 1940 Buick circa 1945. Alva appears to have and apple in his pants pocket. He loved Apples. Grant is about 1 year old.

At the time Alva owned a nearly new 1940 Buick. He could never stop complimenting that vehicle. They truly were spectacular cars. During my career in the automotive industry, I've learned to appreciate them beyond all his compliments. He was driving that vehicle when he met my mother, Gerene Taylor. My Mother told me on several occasions that the Buick was the nicest car that she had ever ridden in. I believe it may have been.

Gerene was working at a textile factory in Malvern while she dated Alva. Gerene drove a 1930 Chevrolet that she had purchased with money she earned. When she and Alva went on a date, they always drove the Buick. Alva told me more than once that the engine was so quite and smooth that often he and my mother would be stopped, talking with the engine idling. Due to the quietness of the engine, he would forget that it was running, release the clutch and stall the engine. Buick engines during that era were noted for their quite and smooth idle characteristics. I was likely conceived in that Buick. I'm not sure what happened to it. I wish I had it today. All I have of it is a photograph of me sitting on the hood. I was about 2 years old sitting there on the radiator grinning while my picture was being recorded.

My first recollections of my life were of my mother, father and me living on a very remote site between Malvern and Hot Springs. I must have been about three years old. The location was on the gravel road that stretched between the two towns and was just inside Garland County. This was a very remote location. The location was known as the 'Bill O'Neal place'.

Grant and Spot

This house was later destroyed by a tornado with us inside

I can remember, vaguely, Alva farming the location, growing huge watermelons that were so large my mother, Gerene, could not drag one from the field in a gunny sack. The weight of many of them exceeded 100 pounds. They were sold by their weight. Alva would weigh them and mark the weight on the skin of the melon. I can remember many of them were in excess of 100 pounds.

True to his roots, Alva was also making whiskey. This site was ideal for it due to it's isolation. It was an old home site with an old but good house, barn and smoke house. We used all of it. We owned a horse and a mule, several pigs and lots of chickens. I was small, about 4 years old. I stuck with my mother everywhere she went whether it was in the field or at the barn gathering eggs and milking the cow we owned. Alva was always either working the field, with Gerene helping and me nearby or he would be working the still he had hidden in the woods nearby. When he was not doing either of those, he would be away in Hot Springs selling whiskey. I can never remember, ever, seeing him sitting around relaxing during this period.

During one of my Mother's evening sessions in which she gathered the eggs from the chicken nests in the barn I was at her side. She would reach into each nest, which was about one foot by two feet in size with straw in the bottom. There were always several eggs in each nest. Some were brown. Some were white. Mom would usually let me get the eggs out of the lower nests. That had happened on this trip. Then she reached into the top nest that could not be seen because it was head high to her. Suddenly, instead of the usual handful of eggs, Mom jerked her hand back and screamed so loud that it rattled my ears. Then she yelled, "Snake" as she fell to the ground while making an attempt me to pull me back. If there was anything Mom was more afraid of than snakes, it probably hasn't been discovered.

All the screaming alerted Alva who was at the house about 40 yards away. He had no idea what was wrong. All he heard was the scream. So he came with the gun. Mom could hardly talk she was so scared. She could hardly get her breath.

Alva kept saying, "Relax. Breathe real slow and then tell me what's wrong."

Mom finally got the words out. "Snake. In the hen's nest. Up there." She pointed to the top nest of the three that were embedded into the wall of the barn.

Alva was excited too. Most of it from running from the house to the barn. He said, "It's probably a chicken snake. I'll get a stick and get it out."

He found a stick that was to his liking. Climbed up on the side the barn far enough he could see inside. Then he hooked the stick under it and flipped it out on the ground inside the barn. Mom screamed again when it landed on the ground.

"It's just a chicken snake." Alva said. "But I'm going to kill it anyway. We can't have it eating all the eggs. Look, it had one in it that it swallowed."

He shot it a couple times. That was where I learned that snakes keep moving after they are dead. In fact after shooting it, Alva got a shovel and cut it into two pieces. Both pieces kept moving. I was fascinated by this. I asked plenty of questions. Alva just laughed.

He said, "Oh, he's dead now even if he's moving. We can't afford to have him eating all our eggs and scaring your mother."

He put his arm around my Mom and we all walked back to the house. Mom was really rattled. Alva carried the eggs in the basket in one hand and looped his arm around the rifle. All was well at the Bill O'Neal place for the time being but Mom had to lay down for a while before she cooked our supper.

CHAPTER SIXTEEN

Mom's Fainting

"I couldn't co'member" Grant Burris age four

After one of those many trips to Hot Springs, Alva returned to our remote house in the woods where my mother and I waited. I was about 4 years old. There were no neighbors for miles in any direction. While he was away, my mother had fainted and fell to the floor. She apparently had suffered this condition once before in Alva's presence. Perhaps I had been warned about this condition but I was too young to recognize the emergency. Much later, Alva insisted that he had given me instructions on what to do if it should occur while he was away. Of course, I was too young to listen and respond appropriately.

I can remember this: Alva arrived and asked, "Where's Gerene?"

I answered, "Her in there kicking around on the floor."

As he jumped out of the car he yelled, "What do you mean?"

I can still remember him jumping the fence and rushing into the house. It's unknown how long she had been in that condition. I believe it was only a few minutes. I hope it was only a few minutes. He dashed some water into her face and she revived almost immediately.

As soon as she was conscious again and the danger was passed, he turned to me and yelled, "I told you what to do if this happened."

Apparently, my Mother had a condition throughout her life that caused her to pass out without warning. We called it fainting. It was never diagnosed. Alva, likely had warned me of it. The warning had gone over my head. A lot went over my head at that age. When he aroused her in the floor, the magnitude of the event began to sink into my small brain.

Alva yelled, "Why didn't you do something about this? I've told you what to do if this happened."

I misunderstood his reprimand. When he reminded me of some instruction set he may have given out prior to this event. I thought he was talking about all the water he had just poured on the floor. It was a real mess. I couldn't recall ever being told what to do if he spilled water on the floor.

Then he said, "Why didn't you put some water in her face?"

My answer was, "I couldn't co'member."

My mispronunciation of the word 'remember' caught him off guard. He began to laugh at my pigeon English. He couldn't stop laughing for a long while. I think some of his laughter was due to the relief of my Mom's return to the living from her emergency. Alva told the story of this event many times and repeated my 'comember' phrase. I was just happy that I didn't get a beating for my forgetfulness.

Grant in door of our 1937 LeSalle at Bill O'Neil House

We seemed to live at this house, the Bill O'Neil place, for a long time. In reality, the time span was only about one year. It is hard to say how long we might have lived there if a tornado had not changed our plans.

CHAPTER SEVENTEEN

The Tornado

"This is going to be bad. We've got to get out." Alva Burris

The afternoon was hot, as usual. I can remember the sudden atmospheric change although I was small. All the sounds stopped. All the birds, all the insects and all the wind stopped. The air suddenly seemed to become heavy. Alva had had some experience with tornados.

He yelled, "Stop! Listen!" He paused for a long moment. He seemed suddenly excited and said, "Get inside, there's a tornado coming. Hurry!"

We dropped everything. We ran from the vegetable field to the house. Alva carried me. Mom kept up easily. It was about 100 yards to the house. We were hustling through the plowed ground and jumping over rows of vegetables.

We had no more than entered the house until everything changed at once. We had not entered a moment too soon. Although it had been sunny when we began the run for the house, the sky turned dark almost at once. It was so dark I think a car would have needed it's lights to drive although it was about mid- afternoon. Immediately, the wind began to blow hard and the lightning began to flash repeatedly. Each lightning strike was followed by a clap of thunder. There was no time delay between the lightning flash and the sound of the thunder. Each blast overlapped the previous. There were multiple lightning strikes overlapping each other. The same applied to the thunder. In nearly the same instant, the rain began to come in hard sheets. It was like a large fire hose being sprayed back and forth across the roof and windows. I could see it all developing and it was happening quickly. Outside, things were going by the windows. There was a loud roar. The word tornado had meant little to me when Alva screamed it in the field. I was beginning to understand. So, this is a tornado? Outside, it looked like pieces of metal roofing going by horizontally. It was. Alva realized, I think, that it was far more severe than he had first imagined it would be. We were in the direct path of a tornado.

Alva yelled, "This is going to be bad. We've got to get out and get into the storm cellar quick." The storm cellar, unfortunately, was located just outside the house and about 20 feet from the back door. The door to it was parallel with the ground and required lifting it up to enter. Alva and Mom began to try to open the back door. At that moment, the wind tore the roof from our house. There was a tremendous crack and the sound of tearing of wood. I looked up and I could see the flashes of lightning through the sheets of rain. The lightning was like a high powered strobe light aimed at us. The flashes were continuous. The rain was very intense but coming down in hard sheets and not a continuous pour. The loud roar, the strobe effect of the lightning and the thunder was like a gun shot near your ear. Frightening doesn't begin to describe it. Their efforts to open the back door were in vain. The sound of the constant thunder blended with the intense roar of the wind was the most frightening weather I'd ever experienced. The air pressure must have made the door stay shut. Two people, together could not open it.

I heard Alva yell, "We're moving. The house is moving. We are being lifted up. Get Grant and hold onto him."

Alva was still trying to get the back door open. I could barely detect our movement. It's the first and only time Alva seemed frightened to me. It was justifiable. I was too little and dumb to be frightened. Both of them were very frightened. It was obvious by the looks on their faces.

The house was lifted over the little structure in the foreground without disturbing it. We were all in the room under the missing roof during the tornado. There was a glass bowl of fresh eggs just behind the missing vertical siding. None were broken.

Roots of a large tree that narrowly missed the car when it fell

To me, it seemed to end rather quickly. It seemed like about 10 minutes. I'm unsure of the exact span of time. As soon as it had subsided a little, Alva herded us outside. It was light again. It had stopped raining just as quickly as it had started. I noticed almost as soon as they noticed it. The house was no longer on blocks. It was no longer supported off the ground. The first thing I noticed was we no longer had a back porch. We didn't need steps to get to the ground. It had been lifted from the blocks, carried over some small structures, moved about 30 feet sideways and deposited directly over the entrance to the storm cellar. It was just luck that we had been unable to reach the cellar for we would have been trapped in the cellar in the dark under the house. Keep in mind, this was all in a very remote area where no one would have searched for days. Trees had been blown from their roots and left laying on the ground everywhere. Some were missing entirely. Those missing were simply gone without a trace. You could easily see the path of the tornado through the woods on the hillside. It looked like a clearing through the woods for a new road. You could also see our roof. It was in the top of some large pine trees about a quarter mile away. Alva said, "Well, there's our roof. Way over there in the top of those pines." Our car was saved from a large tree falling directly onto it by another tree that did not blow away. One of the miracles of tornados that is widely known. Every building on our property was moved to the side. There was a big scrape mark on the ground where each building had been scooted sideways. I will remember that always. We got a few things, some clothes I guess, and got into our car, which currently was a 1937 LaSalle. It started and ran and we began our trip out to the main road. It took a very long time, until long after dark because Alva had to cut trees blocking the road and then use the car in reverse to pull them clear of the narrow road with a rope so that we could pass. Alva did all the sawing by hand. He must have been dead tired by the time we reached the main road which was only slightly wider and was strewn with fallen trees, also. It was near midnight when we finally made it to Alva's sister's house about five miles away where we spent the remainder of the night. We abandoned the crop of vegetables, what was left of it, and the whisky still as well. I think Alva went back later and salvaged as much of the still as he could so that he could begin again in a new location. All those parts he carried, single handedly on his shoulders at night. The larger parts like the pot had to be abandoned.

CHAPTER EIGHTEEN

Life at the Brawley School House

It filled my mouth with hot dry air and made my body light.

Our next home was a old abandoned school house. It was over 75 years old when we moved in. It had only one room with a little stage at the rear of the room and a huge blackboard on the rear wall. The rear portion of the room was stacked with the antique desks that had holes in the writing area for an ink well. I used one to do my school work. This was the school where Alva had gone to school as a child. He reached the fourth grade. At the time I was too immature to image it, but now I realize it must have held bitter sweet memories for Alva. The name was Brawley School. It had been donated to the district by a local philanthropist, George Brawley, when Alva was only a child. The land was donated and perhaps the money to build the school was donated also. That is unknown.

We moved into the school house. We were like squatters. We lived there about 2 years. We paid no rent. We just moved in. Brawley School house was about 5 miles closer to Malvern than the O'Neil house destroyed by the tornado. No one managed the building. It was about 10 miles from Malvern. There was no place to grow a garden. The soil was very rocky. Alva donated all his spare time to constructing a still and beginning to make whisky. Soon he was producing and selling plenty. The area was a perfect staging area. It was remote but on a well traveled gravel road. Alva knew all the backwoods well. After all, he had grown up in this exact area and attended school in this building through the 4th grade. I can remember all of his trips into the woods with the parts of the still. There were many trips. Many trips were made by car into Hot Springs to purchase supplies for the still. Many more to purchase the sugar, yeast and corn chops. He would purchase a different item on each trip to avoid suspicion. In this old school house like the old house before it, there was no electricity, no running water, only an outdoor toilet and two kerosene lamps for light after dark. A big pot bellied stove provided heat in the winter time. The woods were filled with deer. Anytime we needed additional meat, Alva would kill a deer. He killed many. I was too small to shoot so Alva did all the shooting. He was fast with dressing one after the kill. Once my mother decided to time him during the butchering. From the start to finish meant from the time he hung the carcass onto a tree limb until it was gutted, skinned and quartered and placed into tow sacks to carry home. The time was 11 minutes flat. He performed all those tasks with his pocket knife in only eleven minutes. That brings a whole new meaning to the term "fast food".

Since we had no refrigerator or electricity, we could not keep the meat well unless the weather was cold. During the summer, we would use all the meat we could. Mom would can some of it when possible and the rest Alva would try to sell to some of the same people to whom he sold whisky. If they could not afford it, sometimes he would just give them the venison. It was appreciated. Everyone was poor. He didn't want it to spoil and go to waste. Alva had deep values attached to the waste of food. This was especially true of wild game. He preached this to me whenever the opportunity arose or every time an incident caused him to think of it.

Alva preached to me from a young age that I was to never kill anything that I did not plan to eat. The only exception was protection or self defense. He was opposed to wasting fresh game. He wasn't opposed to wasting an 'enemy' if necessary. Many times I saw his survival mode morality in action. Alva was both ashamed of his behavior and proud. Another enigma. An enigma within a paradox. Alva wanted me to follow his guidance without questioning it. Yet, he wanted me to behave differently than he. He wanted both without me questioning his reasons. Any question I might pose regarding his philosophies was certain to bring out his wrath. And I was always full of questions which usually related to his underlying principles. Then he would get out his razor strap. I would get six to eight licks with that double belt that was about three inches wide. God, did that ever hurt. The bruises would still be visible a week later. Alva called this "teaching me not to talk back".

The wounds from the whipping that I received healed. The memories of them remain. One particular whipping was the worst of all and I still believe it was uncalled for. Here's how it transpired:

Alva, Mom and I were driving the dirt roads between Malvern and Hot Springs looking for deer to shoot. We were driving the 1937 La Salle that the tornado had spared when we were nearly blown away back at the Bill O'Neal place. In the backseat and underneath me was a 12 gauge Lefebvre double barreled shotgun. The shotgun on this day was Alva's weapon of choice for killing a deer. It was nearly always in the backseat, regardless of where we were going. It was always loaded. It had been carried in the back seat for so long that all the blued coating was worn away. The Damascus barrel was bright from wear and the texturing was very artistic. Unknown to me, the safety on the shotgun was inoperative. I think it had always been movable but non functional. That meant it could be fired in either position, safe or fire. I had grown bored with the ride. I was looking for something interesting. I was the typical inquisitive kid. I noticed and took interest in the double triggers on the double shotgun. The geometry of the second trigger had previously escaped my interest. One trigger pointed nearly straight down and was slightly curved. The second trigger was very interesting. It extended far back behind the first trigger to allow the finger to access it. This is a normal design for older side by side shotguns. It was fascinating to me. As I studied it, I noticed that for it to operate it must be pulled to the rear of the gun by the finger and, simultaneously, must be moved straight upward to activate the mechanism inside the gun. The first trigger's movement path was obvious. The second trigger's movement baffled me. I put my finger on it and thought about its, seemingly, impossible path that it must make. How could it move backwards and upward at the same time? I never remember moving the trigger. All I can remember is a sound so loud that I didn't register it. It was as though the car was suddenly filled with smoke and my ears were ringing. I didn't know what had happened. I was confused. I was certain that I had not moved the trigger and even if I had, how had the gun fired if the safety was on? Well, the safety was inoperative. I think Alva was totally unaware of the malfunctioning safety at that time. In addition, the gun had a 'hair trigger'. That meant that the slightest touch on the trigger (like a hair) could fire the gun. This could have been the result of wear or a modification that had been made somewhere in its life. It is unknown. Today, it had fired by me simply looking at it, or so it seemed to me. I had done little more than breathe on it.

Both Alva and my Mother yelled, "What did you do?"

I could barely hear them because my ears were ringing so severely. My eardrums were responding to the extreme pressure that had been applied to them.

I was unaware the gun had fired. I was yelling, "What happened, what happened?" I couldn't hear myself yelling.

Now, I could see the large hole in the right rear quarter of the car. I could see completely to the outside of the car through the hole. It was big. I could see the rear tire through the hole.

Alva had recovered from the blast. Anger had replaced his surprise. Lots of anger. While I was confused from the blast, he stopped the car, opened the rear door and pulled me from the car by my hair. I was five, maybe just turned six. He drug me by my hair around the back of the car to the passenger side where he threw me onto the ground. I did not know what was to come but the thought of it filled my mouth with hot dry air and made my body light. With a quick movement he pulled his pocket knife, which he always kept very sharp, from his pocket. In one quick movement he cut a limb from a nearby tree. He grabbed me again as I'd started to get up. He grabbed me this time by the arm. His grip was like a vise. He beat me with the limb that he had cut until he wore the limb out and it broke. This sounds rapid now as I tell it. In life it seemed to take forever. I couldn't get away from his grip. I was crying, I'm sure, but I don't remember it. Just the pain and the fear of what might happen next. All I can remember was the continuous licks with the limb. I was trying to run from the stick but I was only going in a circle. Round and round we went. I don't know how many times. Finally, that limb gave up and broke. Alva let me go. I fell on the ground. Alva was out of breath but at the time, I hardly noticed because I was thinking of myself . My pants and shirt had protected my bare skin from cuts from the limb but my arms had not fared so well. The backs of my arms were bleeding. The pain from the back of my legs and backside were so severe that I hardly noticed the blood. I lay on the ground while Alva cussed me and rested. That's when I first realized how out of breath he was. I cannot remember or guess how many licks I received. It was enough to wear out a good sized limb from the tree. It was enough to wear down a grown man. During the rest, my Mother stayed her distance but encouraged Alva to let her help me up so that we could all go home. Alva continued to cuss me and threaten what he should do to me. All the threats pertained to my lifespan. Finally, he got his breath and seemed to recover. His first movement was to walk over and kick me. He kicked several times. I was rolling on the ground but unable to get up. The kicks came so fast. My poor Mother was begging him to stop. She didn't dare to touch him for fear he would turn on her. I can't remember the number of kicks. I tried to roll away but he easily caught up with me. All the kicking was sufficient to wear him out again. I was trying to regain my breath knocked out of me by the kicking. Many of them caught me in the side under the ribs. He could hardly cuss me because of his heavy breathing. He went to a nearby tree and cut another limb. This one he took more time to cut all the branches from so that it was like a short whip. My Mother was begging him by now.

She said, "Please don't whip him anymore."

I remember her begging him over and over through all that was happening. She appealed to his fear of being arrested by the police if one should come by. He paid no attention. He was in a rage. He cut the limb and trimmed it to the exact length he wanted. Although he was breathing hard, he came over to me and picked me up off the ground by the hair of my head. He began beating me again across the arms and back and butt and legs. Everywhere. He hit me many times but I cannot remember how many. He was cussing me and hitting me with my Mother begging him to stop. I'm sure I was screaming but I don't remember crying out. All I can remember is wishing it would stop and then another hit with the whip. Again, we were going in a circle. I was trying to escape the licks. He was trying to get another good shot at me. The limb had broken again but he was using what was left of it. The remaining piece was thicker and did more damage when it hit. Circling, circling like a scene from a horror movie. He just kept hitting. He beat me like he hated me. Between breaths when he had the energy to speak he yelled how much he hated me and wished I was dead. I felt he might achieve his goal if it continued. He was holding me by my hair. Apparently, the perspiration from my head and his hand caused my hair to slip from his hand. Or, perhaps my hair came out of my head. My head felt as if my hair had been pulled out. I was too crazed to notice. Either way, he lost his grip on my hair.

I fell on the ground. He gave me a kick while I was going down that sent me near the thick brush. I saw the darkness of the thick brush. My adrenalin must have kicked in, finally. When I hit the ground this time, I was in a wild state myself with self preservation the only program running in my little brain. I saw the thick brush and the darkness underneath and, like an animal pursued, I stayed on my hands and knees and I crawled into the thick brush. I crawled as fast as possible. My crawling speed was sufficient to miss his last kick. The brush was very thick and grew right down to the ground. There was bramble briars, very thick briars growing on the brush and the brush was very thick. It made walking into it impossible. It was like a wall to an upright person. Narrow passage ways had been worn in at ground level by animals. In my effort to hide I had aimed my crawling toward one of the narrow openings. Now, I was an animal seeking safety. I used the path made by rabbits and such to crawl deep into the brush. I crawled until I could not see Alva and my Mother anymore. I crawled until I could see nothing but brush around me exactly like an animal would have done. I could think nothing but, "hide". Escape and hide was all that was on my mind. Nothing else. I could hear my Mother calling, "Come back out Grant. Where are you?" I don't know how long I had laid there, safe, when I first realized she was calling me. I had blotted out all but the thought of being safe, finally.

She would say, "Grant, can you hear me? Answer me if you can hear me."

I said nothing. I lay there in a heap. I was numb. I could hardly feel my fingers or my feet. Dirt and small leaves were sticking to me where I was wet from sweat and blood. For that long moment I planned to never make another sound as long as I lived. I resolved to be so quiet and motionless that I could never be found. I just lay there. I remember the feeling quite well. Gradually, I began to realize that I had been there a very long time. I think I may have been there thirty minutes or more. That's a guess. I may have been there an hour. The sun was bright when this began. The sun had gone down. I realized that I could hardly move my arms and legs. I was stiff and could barely straighten my arms. I could see all the cuts on my arms. It felt as if it was the same on my back and it was. Both arms had so many cuts around the arms and on my hands that not a square inch was untouched. The places I could see were completely covered with cuts. I was unconcerned with the cuts. I was filled with fear. I was completely cried out. I could cry no more. I had no desire to leave the safety of the bramble briar thicket. My breath was finally beginning to settle down. I could detect my Mother's voice from different locations as she attempted to walk around the thicket in an effort to get me to answer. It was very difficult to walk around this thicket of briars. It was impossible for an adult to penetrate it. It was a perfect hiding place for a beaten kid. A long time had passed. It was beginning to get dark. The briar patch that I was in was large and impenetrable.

I remember my Mother saying, "Grant, answer me so that I'll know where you are."

I finally realized that no one could get me in this briar thicket. I just wanted to stay there forever. I was still scared but I wanted to answer my Mother.

Finally, I had the courage to say, "I'm here."

Mom must have walked around the thicket as she continually called to me. Eventually, she said, "Crawl toward my voice so that I can see you."

I began crawling toward her voice slowly. It would have been a tremendous task if I had not been injured. It was very slow work with all the stickers on the briars and the injuries. The stickers were getting me but I hardly felt them. I crawled a few movements at a time with her calling to me constantly. Finally, I could see her through the thicket. She may have seen my movement prior to me seeing her. I was close but I wouldn't exit the briar thicket. I was still in my animal mode. I was truly a hunted, injured animal. I've never forgotten that feeling. It was a unique feeling and I've never visited it again. I remained inside the thicket and could not be convinced to exit. Only my mother was there to encourage me to come out.

She kept repeating, "Alva is in the car. He's said he's not going to whip you anymore. So, come on out."

Over and over, she kept repeating that phrase. Finally, it soaked in enough that I crawled from the briar thicket and she helped pull me out to the clearing. She held me for a long time. I couldn't cry. There was nothing left to come out. She held me and cried and said nice things to me but I can't remember anything she said. I just know it was nice words. I saw the patterns from my bloody cuts on her dress as she shifted her position to hold me more easily. I was in a daze. I was like an animal picked up from the road after being hit by a car. I was little more than road kill. I was alive but I didn't comprehend much else. The feelings that were going through me are still clear to me today, more than 65 years later.

Finally, we started to walk back to the car through the foliage that surrounded the briar thicket. It was nearly dark. I was afraid to get into the car. Every time Alva would move in the car I would try to break free and get away. I didn't want to stray too far from my refuge in the briars. My Mother would hold me tightly by the hand and talk me into continuing all over again. I was like a wild animal. I remember the feeling perfectly.

I was convinced by her to get into the car. My mother sat in the middle of the front seat and I sat beside her by the window. I was glad she was between me and Alva. She had her arm around me but I did not feel safe. We rode that way until we reached the old Brawley School house where we lived. The trip was about 2 miles on the dirt road.

We pulled into the drive and Alva parked the car in the typical spot with the back end uphill so that it could be rolled to a start if the battery failed. Upon parking the car and shutting off the engine, Alva reached over my Mother and grabbed me by my hair again from my position by the door. He pulled me across my mother and from the car. He slapped me with his other hand. As he slapped me he let go and I landed on the ground. He kicked my butt so hard that I slid on the ground. By the time I was getting up he had taken off the belt he was wearing. He grabbed me by the arm and began another beating with the belt. My Mother got out of the car and came around quickly but it was no use. I was on the ground and up and going in that circle, tethered by his grip on my arm again as he hit me.

I'm not sure what my Mother was doing but I vaguely remember her saying, "That's enough, Alva. You've hit him enough. Stop."

He didn't stop. He paid no heed to her requests. He didn't stop until he had worn himself out again. He let go and I fell on the ground. I couldn't stand up. Alva rested till he had his breath back. Then he grabbed me by the back of my pants and my hair. He picked me up carried me up to a brush thicket. He threw me on top of the brush thicket. At least there were no briars in this one. After I landed I was laying on the top of the small trees about ten feet off the ground. I gradually fell down through the limbs until I was able to climb between the limbs and reach the ground. When I reached the ground I ran and crawled to get farther into the woods. It was dark and I could not see very well. So, I didn't go far. I went far enough that I could not see him anymore. I could hear my Mother calling again. I didn't return her calls. A long time passed. Finally, I saw a light. My Mother had found a flashlight somewhere. Maybe it was in the car. The light was dim but I could hear her saying, "Grant. Where are you?" I didn't answer. I didn't know what to do. I knew I was going to stay hidden as long as I could. Finally, she walked close enough that she saw me and quickly reached over to put her arm around me.

I said nothing. I could barely stand up. I had thought I could hurt no more but I was mistaken. I had new scratches and bruises. This time, some of the branches from the trees had poked me in the face as I fell into them on the way to the ground. I'm lucky my eyes were not damaged.

Mom said, "Come on in the house if you can. I told Alva that if he started beating you again, I'd get the gun and shoot him even if he killed me later. Maybe he's finally finished. He got in the car and left. So he's gone for now. It's just you and me. So, come on in."

That made me feel a little better. Mom lead me back to the house, the old school house with one room. I could barely walk. She took me inside. I required help walking up the five or six steps to get in the front door. I couldn't do it alone. Mom used the flashlight to find one of our two kerosene lamps. She lit it with a match that she had on the table. Mom washed me up the best she could and put me in bed. She put some medicine on my arms and back where all the cuts were.

As she doctored me she would frequently just shake her head and say, "I don't know why Alva wants to act like that."

She promised me that she had made up her mind. She said she was going to contact someone as soon as she was in town again and make arrangement to leave him and take me along. She never did. She never followed through. I was about six years old when this happened.

It took a long time to heal from this whipping. Alva eventually came back that night. Perhaps it was the next day. I cannot remember. It was a very traumatic time for me. I missed more than a week of school because of it. I was not able to ride the bus to school. I may have missed as much as two weeks of school. I can't remember exactly. When I finally returned to school, my Mother had me wear a long sleeved shirt so that no one could see all the cuts on my arms. I had many cuts and bruises on my back that were covered by my clothes. Both my eyes were still black but improving. Mom put her makeup on my eyes so that it wasn't so noticeable. The severity of the damage was beyond description. Nearly every square inch of my arms, back and legs were covered by cuts. The backs of my hands were the same. My face had several bruises around the eyes. Those bruises had diminished by the time I returned to school but they were still visible. I can remember the teacher, Mrs. Holt, noticing my wounds when she was near me. She seemed so surprised and asked me to see my arms. I refused to pull up my sleeves so that she could see. Finally, when the recess came and the other kids were out playing, she asked me to raise up just one sleeve so that she could see. I reluctantly did that. She was so surprised. I could see her cringe. She asked if the other arm looked the same. I answered that it looked almost the same.

I answered with a lie. I said, "My dad and I were playing in some briars and I got scratched."

She said, "Is that why you were out of school for a few days?"

I answered, "Yes, Mam."

I think she did not believe me. She asked no more questions. She simply returned to her desk and told me to remain at my desk if I wanted until recess was over. I thought I would get in trouble for telling her a lie. I didn't. So far as I know, nothing was ever done or said regarding that incident. Mrs. Holt was a good teacher. She was nice and I liked her but, to my knowledge, nothing was ever done or said regarding my condition. At the time, I was glad I was off the hook and happy that no one else was asking questions. I knew that if I revealed what had happened I'd surely get another beating.

My mother doctored my wounds at night before I went to bed. They healed up before too long. Alva never mentioned the incident again so long as he lived. Neither did I. Many confrontations followed. Many whippings with the double razor strap. Several were severe. None as severe and lengthy as the one just described. No apology or explanation was ever offered by Alva. Never.

Grant, Alva & 38 lb. turkey at Old School

CHAPTER NINETEEN

Brawley Cemetery

Introspection can be a paradox of it's own

Brawley Cemetery West of Malvern, Arkansas

There was an old community cemetery up on the hill behind the Brawley School house. It was the Brawley Cemetery. Many of Alva's family members were buried there. Sometimes Alva would take an axe and a shovel and go up there and work nearly all day clearing away brush and fixing up the graves so they looked fresher. He would spend the day up there by himself working. I wonder what thoughts were on his mind while he was there. I can imagine. Charlie was buried there. The mere mention of Charlie always brought a tear to his eye. During a visit there once, sixty years later and long after Alva was gone, I purchased flowers from town and placed them on the graves that I knew were meaningful to Alva. I put flowers first on Charlie's grave. I thought for a long while as I stood by Charlie's grave. I thought, what would Charlie think of me and what advice would he have given Alva as an older brother would logically give a sibling.

Charlie Burris Grave at Brawly Cemetery

Would he have said, "Stay away from the whisky business"?

I placed the flowers and thought to myself, "On behalf of Alva, I place these here because he can't. He would if he could." I thought of the violin, the heirloom that Alva treasured that once belonged to Charlie. I thought of how, now, I'm the keeper of that violin that once belonged to Charlie. I've kept my promise to keep and protect the violin. All that Charlie was to his family and to Alva was reduced to an oblong pile of white rocks with a marker at one end. Now someone unknown to Charlie, I, related by blood but more by a legacy, was placing flowers on a pile of rocks on behalf of Alva, someone who was resting under his own personal pile of rocks in a distant cemetery. Is that our destiny? Is it my destiny? If so, who will place the flowers on my rocks and will it matter? I think it will not matter whether my rocks are flowered or not. I did this for Alva because I know it would have pleased him. I believe he would have done the same for me.

Sometimes I'm driven to levels of self-examination which border on guilt but lack the sentence of a conviction or a formal pronouncement of blame. Introspection can be a paradox of it's own. One should proceed with caution in this direction for you may find what you wish not to see. By the same token, the examination of one's self can be productive if the objectivity and sensibility of an aging judge is maintained. So, who can perform in the capacity of an aging judge, I ask?

I have learned much from Alva. Perhaps I have learned as much from his mistakes as from his successes. One thing is certain. I am appreciative of the lessons. Without realizing it, Alva taught me success with his failures. He taught me, unintentionally, that within every failure there lurks a lesson. Time has blurred the failures like inked angry phrases on a paper thrown into the rain. The lessons, the knowledge gained, remain steadfast like chiseled words on a marble monument, standing erect in that same downpour.

CHAPTER TWENTY

Quieter Times at Brawley School

Briefly, I thought I was dead

Not all days at the Brawley School were filled with anger and turmoil. Many evenings when Alva was feeling in a gentler mood he would take out Charlie's treasured violin and begin to play. He knew many tunes mostly of Irish origin. I believe, according to his stories, that he had learned them by attending dances with Charlie. Charlie was frequently the violinist at neighborhood dances when Alva was 8 - 10 years old. If Alva was inspired he would sing the lyrics to the songs he played on that old fiddle. He had a phenomenal memory of song lyrics and poetry. Sometimes, in rare instances, he would sing and dance briefly while he played. The dances were all Irish jigs with the exception of a brief tap dance if he was in the mood. He danced those simple dances well. I enjoyed these moods. All were at night. All were lighted by two kerosene lamps that we kept on either side of that large Brawley School house room. There was a big pot-bellied stove on one side the room that would glow cherry red when a fire was in it during the winter. It was about midway between the ends of the room. A wooden table for our meals was centered in the room. Alva would sit between the stove and the table and begin playing his music lighted by those two lamps with their dim amber light. My Mother would never sing with him although he often encouraged her to do so. She seemed offended that he had asked. It was not unusual for a session like this, that seemed to be going so well, to end with an argument. My mother seemed to have a penchant for criticizing Alva about his music and his singing. He could not perform long until Mom would begin her criticism of him. I never understood her motive for this. It was truly a flaw in her diplomacy. Perhaps her lack of talent caused her to be intimidated by his performance. She could have wrapped him around her finger if she had used the correct words during these episodes. He was soft and vulnerable at these times. Instead, she seemed to build up a head of steam or something. Perhaps she sensed his vulnerability. Soon, she would make a negative comment about his music. If the first comment didn't get his attention, she would say something else. I would just hold my breath because I knew, soon, the fight would begin. Alva seemed so caught up in his music that the first few comments went over his head. He would not respond at first. However, that was short lived. When he realized that she was deliberate with her criticism and trying to be malicious, he would stop playing, lay the violin down or put it away. When he returned to the table area, he would say nothing at first, take a deep breath and often back hand her so hard it would knock her from her chair to the floor.

I could write the script for the rest of the night. Alva had been offended and he didn't get over his angry spells quickly. Mom would lay on the floor crying. Sometimes Alva would kick her once and tell her to get up. She would beg him not to hit her anymore. She would get up and sit in a chair or go sit on the bed that was in the same room just beyond the eating table. Alva was, by this time, on a rant. He would curse her and remind her of everything she had ever done that had made him angry. All her past would be brought to bear. Sometimes she would argue back, lightly. This usually caused more slapping which caused more crying. Me? I was always scared to death during these events. I tried to stay well away from him. Once he was angered, he could easily include me in the discipline process. Often he did. There were more of them that swept me into the melee than I can remember. They all turned out badly.

During one of these events, for reasons I cannot remember, Alva became more enraged than normal. This time, for reasons unknown, he walked to the wall where he kept the Winchester Model 94 30-30 caliber rifle. It was always loaded. All it required to shoot was to cock the hammer. The argument progressed to levels it had never reached before. Alva threatened Mom with the gun and the argument seemed to feed something sinister inside him. Instead of him calming down after repeatedly hitting her across the back and the side of her head with the gun barrel he became more enraged. Somewhere during the argument he sat the gun down with stock on the floor and the barrel against the table. Each of them was making accusations to the other. I was, as usual, trying to block it out with no place to hide in a one roomed school house. The argument escalated and a direct threat on her life must have been made because my Mom jumped up and began running for the only door, the front door, screaming. She was dressed in a thin white gown. She was ready for bed. I saw her jump up and run for the door. From the corner of my eye I saw Alva leap for the rifle. I don't know which happened first. As she ran for the door, Alva grabbed the rifle, aimed it at her and fired. Everything happened in one motion. I saw the blur of motion all around me and simultaneously, the pressure from the rifle blast hit my ears and my body with such force that, at first, I couldn't identify what had happened. The sound of the rifle in the room was so intense that it blew out both the kerosene lamps. It nearly blew out my eardrums. There was the scream from my Mother as she ran for the door, the explosion and then sudden darkness. My ears were ringing. I was terrified. It was so dark that I could see nothing. I could hear nothing, just the loud ringing sound in my head. It was from the blast of that 30-30 Winchester just behind me and to my side. I had no sight. I had no sound. Briefly, I thought I was dead.

Alva quickly struck a match that he always kept in his pocket. That match returned life to the room. I realized that I wasn't dead. From the light of the match, that came from his pocket, he walked to the table and lit one of the lamps. The rifle was cradled in his arm. The room was filled with the smoke from the gunpowder. I could smell it. I could taste a bitter taste in my mouth. I wondered how something bitter got into my mouth. I was unaware of the huge amount of adrenaline that is dumped into our blood stream when frightened, to give our body the strength and intensity we need to either fight or run away. This overdose of adrenaline causes a coppery metallic taste to flood our mouths. The sound, the darkness, the bitter taste all surprised me with the suddenness and frightened me unbelievably. Later, I realized the taste was caused by the fear. Alva began calling my Mom.

One of the lamps from the Brawley School House that was blown out by the rifle shot

Alva said, "Gerene.... Gerene..... Where are you? Come on back in here."

No answer from Mom. I could barely hear Alva calling. Just a loud ringing in my ears. I could smell the gunpowder in the air. When the lamp lit, I could see the haze of the smoke from the rifle. It was like a large blanket that floated half way between the floor and the ceiling. I stood very still. I was afraid to move until Alva instructed me to help him.

He began looking on the floor for blood. He began his tracking mode as if my Mother was an animal he had shot. He told me to help him look. He got the lamp, the one in the picture, and made me look on the floor for blood while he held the lamp close. He didn't trust me to hold the lamp. I looked and tried to comply with his request.

He said, "Do you see any blood? I don't think I hit her. Do you see any blood?"

He was adamant that I look carefully for the blood. I was afraid to resist. I was afraid to look. I was in a daze that bordered between fear, deafness and the urge to run as fast as I could. Where would I run? If I ran, maybe Alva would shoot me too.

I was looking for my Mother's blood on the floor of an old school house in the middle of the woods, miles from any neighbor. My ears were ringing loudly. I was unsure if I would hear again. I was hoping to find blood stains in an effort to please Alva. Whether I found blood on the floor was about to determine whether my Mother had just been killed. The magnitude of the situation wasn't sinking in. I was so dazed by it all that I could not think clearly. I was scared and focused on trying to please him. Years later the paradox of looking for blood and wishing to find it while simultaneously wishing there would be none to be found, registered with me. I was trying hard to find the blood of my injured Mother in an effort to please my Dad. I can remember that night like it was yesterday. I was truly scared and I knew I had no choice but to comply with whatever he requested.

The evening had gone from a musical to a shooting in hardly a blink of the eye.

Alva took the lamp outside to see if he could see any blood out on the steps that led to the front door. We were hunting for blood like trailing a wounded animal. Only this 'animal' was my Mother. There were about 6 steps leading up from the ground to the door. I saw no blood on the steps in the dim light from the kerosene lamp. I was trying hard to find blood. I was afraid of displeasing Alva. Slowly it was sinking into my little brain. My failure to find blood was good. What if he found blood and I didn't? I was sure to get a beating if that happened. I was beginning to realize the significance of my failure to find blood. If I failed to find any, that meant she was not wounded. If I failed to find blood I would likely be whipped for failing to pay attention. This thought was forming in my mind as my hearing, lost to the 30-30 blast, was starting to return.

My Mother was wearing only a thin gown when this started. It was a cool night. Now, if she was unhurt, she was alone in the deep woods with no light, no shoes, no protection from animals that might take their turn with her. Alva began to show signs that he was truly concerned. I believe the thought of what he may have done was beginning to have an effect on him. Common sense was finally seeping back into his enraged brain.

I stood at the base of the steps. He told me to wait there. He put the lamp back in the house and blew out the flame. He returned to the front door, locked it and asked me get into the car with him. He pulled out onto the road, a gravel road, in front of the school house. He began calling to her out the open window of the car as we drove along slowly with the gravel crunching under the tires. He would stop briefly to see if he could hear her answer. There was no answer. Alva drove the road in both directions. Sometimes we would stop, shut off the engine and listen for a long time, then we'd drive along slowly again. We drove up and down the road many times. After a very long time, Alva took me to a house miles up the road from the school house where his sister, Dora, lived with her adult son, Harold. He left me there. It was late at night or early in the morning hours. I can barely remember going in. Aunt Dora was awake. She asked what was happening.

Alva said, "Gerene ran off into the woods and is acting crazy. I've been trying to find her. I can't find her. I thought she might come up here to your house. Maybe. So, I want to leave Grant here if its OK and I'm going to drive the road some more to see if I can see her. If she comes here tell her to stay here and I'll come back in the morning."

Aunt Dora said, "OK. I hope she's alright."

Knowing Alva's ways, Dora, as a parting shot, said, "Alva don't do anything you will be sorry for. You hear me?"

Alva answered, "Oh, no. I won't. I'm just trying to find her."

During the night, my Mother, somehow, made her way from the old school house through the woods without walking on the road. She had been uninjured by the rifle shot. Later she said she had walked the edge of the road and when she saw a car coming, she would run into the woods to hide until it passed. The distance was several miles. She did this without shoes and without a light of any kind. She came to Dora's door and knocked. Dora got up and let her in. I don't know the hour that she arrived.

When I awoke the next morning, I was sleeping between two women. I was between my Mother and Dora. Each had their back turned toward me. I didn't know which one was my Mother. I laid there a long time unable to determine which was which. They were equal in size. Finally, after what seemed to be an hour, but was likely only a few minutes, my Mother turned over a little bit and I discovered, with relief, she was the one on my right. She had a black eye on her right eye. I could see where blood had dried within her eyebrow. I guess it was from one of the licks with the gun butt before Alva shot at her. Her eye was swollen. I was so happy and surprised that she wasn't shot. I told her that I loved her.

I said, "Mom, I love you." And she started crying and hugged me really tight. She held me close for a long time while she sobbed uncontrollably.

The soft sobbing woke Dora and she turned over and said, Good morning, Grant."

Dora said, "Gerene, how do you feel?

Mom said, "OK. Just tired. I don't know if I slept any or not."

They both got up at almost the same time. They had to get up so that I could get up. They had me pinned in. The bed wasn't very big. Dora and Mom talked briefly, then they began to cook some breakfast. I remember the odor of bacon mixed with that of coffee. That odor relaxed me a bit and made the morning seem a sharp contrast to the night before. Harold was not up yet. Soon it began to seem almost normal again. I was sure glad that I was at Dora's house.

Harold, Dora's son, got up said his hello to us. Harold was a quiet and competent man. Breakfast was ready soon and we all ate together. That familiar odor of bacon and coffee was throughout the house. It was more than an odor. It was a feeling and it sure felt good. I was hungry and Harold and Aunt Dora were nice people to be around. They were both easy going people and seldom ever showed any anger. This was a welcome experience after the previous night.

About 10 AM Alva drove up in the driveway. My Mother jumped up and began to attempt to hide. Her disposition did an about-face. She looked for a place to hide and began to cry again. Harold tried to console her. Mom was a woman who had been narrowly missed by a 30 caliber round just a few hours prior. She was running from corner to corner of the room like an abused animal. I wanted to help but I was scared and at a loss as to what I should do. I was about five years old.

Harold said, "I'm going to go out and talk to Uncle Alva. He's not going to hurt you while you are here. Just sit down and relax."

Harold really took charge of the situation. I'd never seen anyone who thought they could manage Alva if he was mad. Harold seemed to know what he was doing. He seemed very confident of himself. His words made me relax a bit.

Harold said, "Uncle Alva is not going to hurt me and I'm going to make sure he doesn't hurt you. So, just sit down and wait 'til I'm finished talking to him. I won't let him come inside until I'm sure it's all OK."

Mom listened to Harold but I could tell she was still scared. Dora sat with her and was trying to comfort her. Mom was very scared. She could not keep from crying.

Harold was outside for a long time talking to Alva. They stood beside the car maybe 15 minutes. They seemed very calm. I watched every move. Then they walked over to some of the out buildings at Dora's house. They talked more and by their movements I thought they seemed pretty normal. Gradually, they moved back closer to the house. When they got back to the gate in the fence that surrounded the house, I heard Harold tell Alva to wait there until he went inside.

I saw Alva nod in agreement but he said nothing.

Harold came in and told us that Alva had apologized to him for the way he behaved the night before.

Harold said, "Uncle Alva said he was sorry for the way he acted and that he isn't going to hurt you. He'd like to come in and talk to all of us if we will let him."

Mom said, "Whatever you all think. I'm dependent on you to keep him from killing me while we are here. There's no telling what he will do when we leave."

Dora said, "Well, you don't have to go with him. You and Grant can stay here if you want to. Why don't you talk to him and then see how you feel about it?"

Mom agreed, reluctantly, to this. So Harold went out and invited Alva to join us.

We all talked. At least the adults talked. I listened. Alva seemed to be in one of the best moods that I can remember. He was like a changed person. I believe he slept, alone in that school house believing he may have killed my Mother. He seemed visibly relieved when he realized, upon entry into the room, that Mom was not injured. Perhaps those thoughts rendered some of the anger from him that night. He was a changed man the next morning at Dora and Harold's house. He was on his best behavior. I was glad but I knew his moods could change quickly.

When we returned to the school house, my first wish was to see where the bullet went since it didn't hit my Mother. What did it actually hit? I found the round hole in the door facing just above where she had exited the building. Forever after that for as long as we lived there, every time I walked through the doorway I would look up at that bullet hole and remember that night again.

CHAPTER TWENTY ONE

Thanks for Faulty Ammo

I spotted a good opportunity to keep my mouth shut as Alva reached for a pistol he kept in the glove box.

All of Alva's anger was not always directed at my Mother and me. He was quite capable of getting pissed at other people too. I can remember one of our trips to Malvern. For reasons beyond the intellectual ability of a kid such as I, a bit of road rage developed between Alva and another driver on the way into Malvern. The first indication that something was about to happen came from a quick turn of our car that sent me flying to the floor from the back seat where I was sitting. Almost in the same instant Alva let loose with a stream of profanity aimed at another driver. I understood little but I knew something was about to happen. My Mother was already well into her "Don't get yourself into trouble mode".

Alva's profane descriptions of the other driver continued. My attention was directed to the car ahead of us. The offending driver had apparently ran us off the road and only Alva's quick response had saved us and the other driver from an accident. We were rapidly catching up with whoever was driving the other car. Alva was rapidly describing the driver's heritage with choice four letter words that he stitched into long sentences.

Soon, we overtook the driver in the other car. There was little traffic. Alva pulled alongside him. My Mother's window was down because it was a hot summer day. Alva screamed at the other guy through the open windows. The other guy screamed back. They each sounded about the same. Alva didn't recognize the guy according to his later recount of the event. The cars weaved from side to side on the two lane road. Each driver was detailing his feelings of the other. No traffic was coming from the opposite direction. That was luck. One expression of the other driver seemed to ring in Alva's ears. The other driver called Alva a 'son of a bitch'. It was just a cliché expression, but Alva took this expression as an assault on his mother. He always did. I had experienced his hatred for this particular remark. It always sent him into another level of anger. This time was no different from the rest.

The other driver's car must have been a little hotter than ours because he hit the gas and away he went ahead of us.

Alva said, "He may have thought he out ran us and has gotten away but I'll catch up with him. I'll catch him and when I do, he will be sorry."

My Mother was well aware of what those words could mean. She didn't waste a second. She began pleading with Alva to just forget about it.

Mom said, "Forget about it and don't let it ruin the day. He was probably drunk and didn't even know what he was saying."

Alva just shook his head as if to shrug off the warning. He was mad. We slowed down and drove normal as we entered Malvern. We rounded the turn on Moline Street as it became Main Street from there on into Malvern downtown. There is a hill just before entering Malvern from the east. It's named Baker Hill. Along the side is a nice spring. Or once was. Maybe the spring is called Baker Spring. I don't know the name. It was a nice spring with a concrete container holding lots of water. You could use the water in the large container to fill thirsty automobile radiators or you could catch the fresh water from the pipe if you wanted a cool drink. Just as we topped Baker Hill, Alva spotted the car we had been chasing. He was pulled over at the spring. The driver was at the wheel. Mom spotted it at the same time as Alva. I spotted a good opportunity to keep my mouth shut as Alva reached for a pistol he kept in the glove box.

Mom launched her last futile barrage of warnings filled with, "You'll be sorry you didn't listen to me."

Alva paid no attention. He was on a mission to salvage his mother's verbally threatened character. And to win this altercation one way or the other.

Mom said, "Alva, don't take the gun."

Alva said, "He might have one. I want to be prepared."

He was mad. We had a ring-side seat. We were parked slightly to the side and to the left rear of the car at the spring on the hillside. Alva walked up to the car and his first words were, "You thought you got away didn't you?"

I couldn't hear the other guy but he said something to which Alva said, "I'm going to give you one chance to apologize for how you drove and what you said. You risked our life and your sorry life by driving that way."

Something happened within the guy's car. The window was down. Alva had the pistol at his side in his right hand. His left fist was clenched. Alva's left hand moved fast. It hit the guy twice, maybe three times, so quick I couldn't count them. He hit him through the open window. With the last jab he grabbed the guy's hair and jerked him half out the open window. He put the gun to guy's head right behind his ear and pulled the trigger. It all happened in one motion, so it seemed to me. As he pulled the guy's head out the window, my Mother, sensing what was going to happen, screamed just as I heard the hammer click.

Being young, I couldn't follow the action and read it like an adult. My Mother was following every move and knew a split second before the climax just what was going to happen. She likely saw the gun movement beginning before it reached the side of the guy's head.

I heard the click of the hammer falling on the chamber. I was too young to comprehend the magnitude of the situation. It seemed like time froze. I think time really did freeze for a moment. I remember the sound of the click, then the gun still behind the ear, then my Mother let out this loud breathe of air mixed with a moan of relief. I think it was relief. Alva stood there with the guy's hair in his left hand, the gun in his right hand, the tip of the barrel against the guy's head. It was a long moment. My mother didn't breath for that long moment. Time froze.

Then Alva hit the guy across the head with the gun barrel twice, hard. He left him hanging out the window with the blood dripping down and some running on the side of the car. I watched the guy hanging from the window of his car, bleeding on the ground and on his car's door as we drove beside him and reentered the street. I was about three feet from him as we drove by. Somewhere in that time Alva returned from the fight scene, got back into our car, started the engine and we drove by as we went down Baker Hill and into Malvern. Time seemed to move so slowly as we drove by. I can remember the blood dripping off the man's hair onto the door of his car. It was running down in one stream all the way to the bottom of the car. I was the only one looking at him as we drove by. I never knew the man's identity.

The round that was in the pistol failed to fire. The revolver had six rounds in the chamber. The one under the hammer failed to fire. Alva said later that he had gotten too mad that day. He admitted it.

Alva said, "I felt that once again God had prevented me from doing something terrible. That gun had never failed to fire. Yet, that day, that bullet snapped and failed. It had to mean something. I'm glad it turned out the way that it did. He was a smart alec and drunk to boot, but I just got too mad."

The force of the pistol barrel hitting the guy's head warped the frame of the gun. The cylinder would never rotate again. Alva sold it to Vance's Pawn Shop in Hot Springs located between

Central Avenue and Malvern Avenue. I saved that failed round. I still have it in my mementos. The cap is dented properly and deeply by the firing pin of the pistol. Outwardly, it appears to be a round that was fired. However, the projectile remained in the casing. I have looked at it many times as I grew up. Every monumental event carries a lesson. In this instance, it means that sometimes a failure is a good thing. It also means that every day the guy lived following this event was a miracle. People say each day we live is a gift. That is certainly true of the guy at the spring on Baker Hill. Death declared a Mulligan on his life that day.

CHAPTER TWENTY TWO

Shootout Downtown

"He's crazy. He's got a pistol. I shot him and he's trying to get away." Alva Burris

As I reminisce, there seems to be a lot of times that differences were settled with guns. In the episode that I'm about to reveal, a gun was the most practical tool to use. After all, when threatened with a gun the proper defense is a bigger and better gun. Sometimes "a better gun" means simply a gun in the hands of someone who can use it properly.

After the incident at the school house where Alva nearly killed my Mother, and following the incident on Baker Hill, he had behaved himself very well. I believe that shook him up sufficiently to instill some reason into him. That was good. His violence was directed toward us less frequently. That was especially good. Instead, we had many pleasant trips to other towns. We visited with relatives that I hardly knew. That was rare. Alva's income from the whisky was sufficient that we could travel around easily. Our trips included many to Hot Springs and Little Rock and a few to Malvern like the following one. Alva had expressed a desire to purchase some property in Malvern and build a home there that was more modern than the school house. He had mentioned that it would be closer for me to attend school without the long bus ride that I hated so much. Often, when in Malvern, we would look for locations that was affordable for us. Alva wanted to purchase a lot and construct a house on it.

We, my Mother, Alva and I, drove into Malvern from the old Brawley School house place. We went to town for my mother to do a little shopping for a dress she was making. Alva wanted to visit with a local mechanic, Halley Effird. Alva and Halley had been friends for years. Their families were friends in a generation before them. Halley ran a small garage on West Page Avenue which was only a short distance from the center of town. Halley repaired small items on our car when it was needed. Frequently, Alva would visit with Halley while my mother sat and crocheted. I was in the back seat. On this particular day, Alva, with his back to the street, talked to Halley as Halley worked on a car just within his shop. Our car was parked at the curb just a few feet away from the conversation.

Suddenly, a large black man wearing a heavy black (looked black) Navy coat (in summer) walked up behind my dad as he stood talking to Halley. He grabbed Alva by the left arm and spun him around. Alva recognized him. It was Joe Cook. Cook, was a local guy who some thought to be crazy. He likely was. Cook, earlier, had been charged and convicted of attempted murder of his mother. He cut her throat from ear to ear. The story was well known around our small town. Our family knew the Cook family and the various brothers and sisters. Most were between 15 and 30 years old. Joe Cook was one of the oldest. We were well acquainted with all the members of the family, all of whom were nice. I had enjoyed going their house and especially enjoyed the mother whose life had been nearly taken by her son. She had, on one occasion showed me her scar on her neck where the attempt on her life was made. I think, prior to this day, I'd never seen Joe Cook. I'd only heard the story of him trying to kill his mother. That had shocked me but not like I was about to be rattled.

Guns were always a part of our life as I grew up. It was a different world then. We normally carried a shotgun in the back seat of the car, loaded. On this day, Alva had loaded it with #4 shot so that he could shoot at a hawk that had been seen catching a farmer's chickens along our path to town. Alva had hoped to get a shot at him and stop the hawk from robbing the farmer, with whom he was acquainted, of his chickens. This was not an uncommon deed. To have a concerned neighbor take out a hawk for you was considered a great favor. The gun loaded for the job was still in the back seat in case we saw Mr. Hawk on the way home. The gun was a Browning 12 gauge automatic, plugged magazine, with three rounds in it.

When Cook spun Alva around facing him, Alva recognized him at the same time he saw Cook's left hand pull back his Navy coat revealing a Colt 45 automatic pistol in a cross draw position. Cook reached for the Colt 45 auto as he yelled some profanity. The profanity was loud enough that it drew my attention from the back seat through the open window. It wasn't the words. It was the volume of his threat. They were only about 10 feet or less from me and my mother in the car at the curb. It was only the width of the curb. Alva was about 55 years old. He was in great physical condition and as quick as a cat on his feet. When

Cook reached for his gun with his right hand, Alva grabbed Cook's right shoulder with his right hand and gave him a hard pull forward on his right shoulder that make Cook spin counterclockwise. Alva's pull on Cook's shoulder was so strong that Cook had to forego drawing the 45 momentarily while he recovered his fall with both hands to the fender of the car Halley was repairing. Cook was a big man. He was linebacker size. Nearly twice Alva's size. With the same pull Alva launched himself to our car. To me, it seemed that Alva just suddenly appeared at the door. I'd hardly had time to absorb the intensity of what was happening. I knew when Alva moved fast, hell was about to be unleashed. Alva jerked the door open, grabbed the Browning 12 gauge from the seat. It was loaded for hawks but it was about to be emptied on a fresh target. Alva yelled at my Mother and I to get down.

"Get down! Get down!", he yelled.

He didn't have time to check out whether his orders had been followed. He knew that Colt 45 was going to open up any second. It would be aimed straight at us in the car. All of us. Even a near miss could be catastrophic. It held nine rounds if fully loaded.

I didn't get down. I needed to see what was happening.

Alva was too busy to enforce the instructions. The Browning flashed out from under me and up into action. If quail flushed when bird hunting, Alva would typically get a double with the first shot and at least a single with the final shot. Three with two shots was normal for him even with the brush cover afforded upland shooting in Arkansas. He was a great wing shooter. Cook had no idea what he had bitten off. Alva was formidable with a shotgun. Quick and accurate. He just didn't miss. Cook must have had a slight change of heart. All this was happening in micro seconds. Seemed like time was slowed down as it was happening. My eyes were in the open rear door window. I was absorbing every instant of it. My mind was processing the information faster than it was happening. I was oblivious to the danger. I was soaking in the action.

I saw Cook glance toward the car as he recovered from the spin Alva gave him. He had the 45 out of the cross draw holster on his belt by then and was turning toward us. He seemed to turn slowly but he was likely recovering his balance after the spin Alva put on him. The flash of his eyes I'll never forget. All I can remember of him was those eyes and the end of that 45. The hole in that barrel was coming up fast. I was experiencing something called 'tunnel vision'. I was anticipating the blast from the pistol. Something must have clicked in that deranged pea brain of Cook's. He must have seen the flash of that Browning coming out and he chose to run with his 45 still in his right hand. He had had a change of heart. He was a ball carrier on the 20 going for a touchdown. Those big knees were pounding the pavement. Hard.

He was nearly 20 yards down the sidewalk in a full run with arms and legs pumping and that 45 visibly going up and down in his right hand when the first round from that Browning hit him in the back. Time remained slowed for me. It was surreal. I still remember the minute delay between the explosion of the gun and the impact of the shot on his coat. Too brief to measure except in my mind. The blast was, boom. Then, whomp, as the shot hit his coat a microsecond later. The blast hit Cook right between the shoulders. That Browning had a strange pattern. A half dozen # 4's were later picked out of Cook's ass. The dust boiled off that old Navy coat like you had hit a dusty rug with a shovel. The impact knocked him forward about 5 yards and flattened him but didn't kill him. That big thick Navy coat had protected him some from the #4's fired from an open cylinder barrel.

He crawled behind a big oak tree that was to his left between the sidewalk and the street curb. Seemed to me like he was crawling when he hit the ground. Cook's hands and feet were moving before he hit the ground. Alva stood ramrod straight in the middle of the sidewalk. Gun at the ready against his shoulder. If he had been at a skeet range, the next sound heard would have been, "Pull". Cook put the barrel of the 45 pistol up beside the tree on the street side to shoot and Alva instantly put a load right into the area where the end of Cook's gun barrel rested. The bark and wood flew from the tree into the street. The pistol disappeared. A momentary pause. Alva is standing straight, ready for the next shot. Halley Effird crawled into the engine compartment of the vehicle he was repairing. Cook still had a grip on the 45. The gun appeared on the other side, the sidewalk side of the tree. Alva put another load there. Instantly. The blast blew the bark and wood from the tree and it covered the sidewalk.

Alva was counting the shots. He knew he was out of ammo. This was the first break of his stance. Almost as he shot, he spun around and yelled for my Mother to get the buckshot from the glove box of the car. She wasn't fast enough.

He yelled, "Gimme' the buckshot! Gimme' the damn buckshot!"

Mom was digging in the glove box. She got it and he grabbed it. She handed him two rounds. It really only took a heartbeat. Things were happening really fast now. Halley, the mechanic, had crawled completely into the engine compartment of the car he was repairing. All I could see was his cap barely visible over the fender. Now, I glanced and saw his hand reach out and pull the hood down on himself. Halley was fully inside the engine compartment. Alva loaded quickly. It was just click, click. Just two rounds went in the magazine. He clicked the bolt release with his right hand that sent a round of buckshot into the chamber as he raised the gun with his left. All was performed with one smooth quick motion. To a casual observer it appeared he had lowered the gun slightly with his left hand and quickly raised it back on target. One could hardly detect the two rounds of buckshot inserted as he lowered and raised it. Alva watched Cook leave the tree, wounded and hobble down the sidewalk running but slower than before. Alva had reloaded without taking his eyes off Cook who was taking advantage of the break in shooting. Almost fully reloaded, he leveled on Cook again. This is it for Cook. Buckshot are fatal at 100 yards. Cook was about 50 yards away. One of the 38-caliber pellets from the 12 contained in 12-gauge shell can be fatal. At Cook's range most of the 12 pellets will hit his back. Alva had dropped many deer at greater range than this. I'd seen him do it. That's why they call it buck shot. I knew when I heard the sound of the next shot, Cook was going down permanently. No more lucky trees for Cook. No more thick coats. As Alva took aim on Cook, he paused. Gun was in position but he didn't fire. I was expecting a blast from that Browning but none came. Just as I looked from Cook, expecting to see him go down again, I glanced to Alva who was lowering the gun.

Alva yelled, "Damn it. Those people are on the other side of him. If I shoot some of the shot might hit them."

Alva was mad.... oh, was he mad. But, he wasn't too mad to notice a family of people who were about 60 yards beyond Cook.

They were oblivious to what had just happened. They were looking at some cars on a Pontiac dealership lot that was directly beyond Alva's target. I studied this scene later after I was an adult. Alva was incredibly observant to notice them beyond his target and pause as he did.

Alva was wound up. His hackles were up. He threw the shotgun in the front seat with the barrel on the floor and jumped in behind the wheel. He burned the tires as he went down the street and turned right at the corner where he'd seen Cook disappear.

Alva kept saying, "I should have had the buckshot in the damn gun. I always have it loaded with buckshot except this morning because of that hawk. If I'd had the buckshot, I'd have got him with the first shot."

We rounded the corner and confronted a row of 'shotgun' style houses on the right. Alva jumped out with the Browning loaded with buckshot this time. He jumped onto the porch believing that Cook had entered one of the houses to hide. Alva didn't know who lived there. He pounded on the door. Someone answered. There Alva stood at the front door, in a rage, with his shotgun.

Alva said, "Have you seen Joe Cook? You're not hiding him are you?"

The man said, "No sir. We've heard of Joe Cook and we don't like him. He's for sure not hiding here."

Alva seemed to feel a need to warn the stranger in the door. Alva said, "He's crazy. He's got a pistol. I just shot him and he's trying to get away."

Alva yelled at my Mother, "Gerene, see if you see any blood on the sidewalk so I will know which way he went."

Alva didn't wait for an answer. He jumped the fence and went to the next house. The houses were elevated off the ground on blocks. It was typical for that area. Shotgun houses on blocks. Alva was looking underneath the houses like you'd look for a lost dog. He jumped onto the porch and went through the same routine. Pounded on the door. "Where's Joe Cook?" The same at the next house. By now my Mother was yelling at him to come back to the car. She slid over under the wheel and started the engine. She crept forward to stay adjacent with him as he searched the houses one after the other. Alva ran out of houses and he was starting to run out of steam. My mother told him over and over to come get in the car. Alva is unsatisfied. He wanted old Joe Cook. He's mad and he wanted him bad. Now, he has the ammo he wanted but he can't find him. Finally, he gave up and got back in the car. My Mother drove the car and we headed for home.

Alva is aware that he will likely be arrested for this. He wanted to calm down and he wanted some time before talking to anyone about it. So, we got out at our house and he left in the car. After a while, the sheriff came to our house. He asked if Alva was there.

My Mother said, "No sir, he's gone at the moment".

Sherriff took a long pause and said, "There's been a shooting in Malvern and Mr. Burris was apparently involved. So, when you see him, tell him to come on in because it will go a lot easier on him if he does. Will you tell him that?"

My Mother said, "Yes, I'll tell him as soon as he returns."

Alva returned later that night. The following morning we went into Malvern. Alva spoke with someone who could act as a bondsman if he needed such a service. Then he spoke with an attorney who would be handling the case when it came to court. Following that, he went to the sheriff's office and was taken into custody. Alva wasn't required to go to jail although he was arrested. They just did the paper work. Since he had the bondsman there to go his bail, there was no reason to lock him up. We all went home together. I was happy Alva didn't have to go to jail.

CHAPTER TWENTY THREE

The Trial

"I have never seen so many bullet holes in a guy that was still walking." unknown

A few months passed before Alva was required to appear at the trial. The story of the shoot out on West Page Avenue had spread. The newspaper ran a story on it. That launched the secondary stories which exceeded the real story. The story got bigger by the week.

By the time the trail was scheduled, there was a tremendous crowd to watch it. I remember asking my Mother why so many people were there. I'd never seen so many people. She answered that many people were there to see what would happen to my daddy. That scared me. I began to wonder what would happen too.

City Hall Malvern, Arkansas. Upper Floor was Used as a Courtroom for Burris/Cook Trial The entire lawn around the building and most of the street was filled with people

Alva had an attorney that he trusted. His name was Jim Cole. Cole exuded intelligence. Cole had two brothers. One was a pharmacist and owned a pharmacy in town. The other was a local doctor. Jim was tall, slim and wasted no words. When he spoke, he commanded attention. He was an excellent listener. Therein lay his strength. When the date for the trial arrived, Alva insisted that I be allowed to sit up front with him for the experience. I was happy to do so. I can't remember all the text of the trial. I wish I could. It was interesting. I can remember only a portion of it.

Attorney Cole cross questioned Cook on the stand. The line of questioning was somewhat like this.

"Mr. Cook what did you have in your hand the day of the altercation?"

"I had a knife"

"Now, Mr. Cook we have testimony from eye witnesses who say that you were pointing something at Mr. Burris. Other eye witnesses testify that they saw you with an object in your hand. Do you deny that?"

"No"

"What I'm going to ask you is, if you say that all you had in your hand was a pocket knife and eyewitnesses testify that you were pointing the object in your hand, whatever it was, at Mr. Burris, and other eyewitnesses say that you were pointing an object in your hand at Mr. Burris from behind the tree, then I'm going to ask you, why would a grown man be pointing a pocket knife at another man from behind a tree?

The courtroom roared with laughter. The court and the spectators were quickly on Alva's side. The attorney, Jim Cole, earned his pay in fine style with a few more jabs such as the one I remembered. In the end Alva was acquitted. The ruling was that it was self-defense. Alva was free. It seemed to me it was over. However, it was not.

Alva was perceptive. He noticed that Crazy Cook was wearing the same coat that he was wearing the day of the shooting. It was not difficult to identify the coat as the same one. The coat had bullet holes all over it. You could see daylight any direction you looked through it. I had heard people behind me laughing about it. Plus, Cook had obvious shotgun pellet scars covering each side of his face.

Behind me I heard one man say, "I have never seen so many bullet holes in a guy that was still walking."

The local stories have it that over 100 shot were picked out of Cook's back, butt and face with one pellet located directly between his eyes.

Alva, realizing how crazy this Cook guy was, went to the bailiff after the trail was over and while everyone was in the courtroom. Everything was in a state of semi-celebration. The entire room seemed to be on the side of Alva, the defense.

Alva said to the bailiff when he reached his side, "This Cook guy is crazy. He's wearing the same big coat that he wore the day I shot him. It's summer. It's not a cold day. I'll bet he's carrying that 45 Colt right here in the courtroom. Why don't you check him and find out?"

The bailiff said, "You could be right. It looks suspicious. It won't hurt to check him."

In those days, no one was searched before entering the courtroom. There were no rules in that regard. There were no metal detectors. Half the room could have been wearing weapons and no one would have known. They searched Cook. Alva was right. Crazy Cook was wearing the Colt 45 auto cocked and locked right in the courtroom during the trial. All the time he was being questioned on the stand he had a cocked 45 automatic in his belt with a round in the chamber. Truly crazy. We were truly lucky. The entire courtroom was lucky.

Cook was disarmed, handcuffed and taken to a jail cell on the spot with the crowd watching. The recent turn of events traveled fast. That increased the tempo of the stories about the shooting even more. The crowd had gotten what they came for. Alva was an overnight celebrity.

The story spread quickly. Maybe more quickly in the black community because Joe Cook was black. Following this trial, and before his arrival at any destination, everyone seemed to know Alva. His reputation preceded him. Often I watched as he would go to a house. As he stepped onto the porch, people would come from the house and begin shaking his hand. The residents of a house would summons their neighbors. Soon there was a crowd circling Alva.

"Why didn't you kill old Joe Cook?" was a common question.

They would all laugh and want to engage Alva in a short conversation. Most hated Cook for what he had attempted on his Mother.

I can hear the comments now. "Mr. Burris, they say that he was shot in his back, shot in his face on the right, shot in his face on the left, shot in both his hands, shot in both his arms, shot in his butt and they say he was standing behind a tree the whole time you was 'ah shootin' him. I wants to know. How one man can shoot another man all ovah' while that man's behind a tree? Do you have some kind of special gun that shoots around trees and around corners? I wants to know how you did that."

All would laugh. Especially Alva. He appreciated their acceptance of what happened. He felt vindicated.

During that period Alva paid a visit to his friend's place in Hot Springs, the Harris Funeral Home. Mr. Harris had been a close acquaintance of Alva for years. He was an occasional whisky customer. Mr. Harris was a nice man. He was educated. I always enjoyed stopping at their place when we were in Hot Springs. He seemed intelligent and composed. At a young age those qualities impressed me. They still do.

Mr. Harris looked at Alva midway through one of their conversations which naturally strayed to the shooting on West Page Avenue. Mr. Harris looked at Alva and paused for dramatic effect.

He said, "Mr. Burris, why didn't you just kill that crazy Joe Cook and be done with it. He tried to kill his own mother one time. He cut her throat from one side to the other. Only thing saved her was her daughters held the blood vessels til they got to the hospital. She's still got the scar. Nobody would've done nuthin' if you had just killed him and walked away."

Alva answered, "Well, Mr. Harris, I tried to, but I had the wrong shells in the gun that day."

Mr. Harris just smiled and said again, "Nobody would've done nuthin'."

Alva liked Mr. Harris. He repeated that phrase many times. Nobody would have done nothing. He felt justified for what had happened. For certain, he was well known for it.

CHAPTER TWENTY FOUR

Trips to Malvern

I've seen worse than this at home. Grant Burris

Some of the folks that bought whiskey had neighbors that were interesting. Alva would gather information about the surrounding neighborhood when he was interrogating a new customer. Likely questions were, "Who lives next door to you? What do they do for a living? How many people live in the house?"

This was typical. It was just good business to know the adjacent neighborhood. Along with acquiring the statistics of the neighbors, Alva often dug up other interesting facts. In one case, Alva told my Mother and I after we had returned home one evening that the house near where we had been parked that afternoon while in town was occupied by a group known to the locals as the 'Nightfighters'.

Alva said, "I never knew this before. The house across the street from where we were parked has a family living there who begin fighting with each other every night as dusk begins to fall."

My Mother questioned this. She asked, "Do they fight with each other or with their neighbors?"

Alva said, "Irene, the lady I was talking to in her house, said they never bother their neighbors. They only fight with each other. There is about ten or twelve who live there. Irene said they sleep all day and every evening as it begins to get dark, they come out of the house and begin wandering around outside. They act as though they had just woke up. Maybe that is why they are not seen much during the daylight hours. Anyway, Irene said they come out at night and slowly begin to engage each other."

Alva continued, "Irene said they put on a real show and that we should come back some evening and watch them."

I had never heard of anything like this. Apparently, neither had my Mother or Alva. We agreed that some evening soon, we would return and watch. We all agreed that it would interesting.

True to the promise that we would return, Alva suggested the next day that we should go into town from our school house home and watch some night fighting.

We arrived at the spot near where they lived. We parked the car in spot that Alva believed would give us the greatest view point. It was not yet dark. We had picked up some sandwiches from a local barbeque cafe. I couldn't wait to see what would happen. After a short time I grew bored. I busied myself with something I had carried. I had nearly lost interest in the entire affair when I heard Alva say, "There's one coming out of the house."

I looked over the seat. One man was walking out the front door. The house was poorly kept and not large. Suddenly, the man jumped a few steps forward and opened the gate that emptied onto the dirt road where we were parked. The reason that he had jumped forward was likely due to something said by a person in the house. Almost immediately, I saw a lady, a large lady in the door way of the house where the man had walked out. She was talking but I couldn't hear her well. She was addressing the man who had walked out in front of her. She wasn't happy. That was clear. The man walked onto the street, perhaps fifty yards from our car. The argument was obvious but we couldn't understand a word they said. The man began walking up the road in front of our car and toward us.

Alva said, "If they come by here, just be quite and pay no attention to them. There's no telling what they will do."

The man kept walking in the direction of our car while the woman slowly pursued him. The argument continued with most of the dialogue coming from the woman. Soon the man was nearly even with our car. He was about even with our left front fender. Suddenly, without warning, he began running. At the same time, the woman began to run also. It appeared the argument had heated up due to words exchanged between them. The man began running with the woman maybe twenty yards behind. They, one by one, came right by our car as though they had not seen us. The chase continued until we could hardly see them behind us. Almost simultaneous, as they passed the car and with my attention on them, Alva redirected our attention to the house where they lived.

Alva said, "Look at that."

A man was crawling out one of the side windows and a woman came out the back door with a man in pursuit. My head was spinning. I had lost sight of the couple behind the car and there was plenty happening up front. The man became violent with the woman in the back yard immediately. He caught her quick and knocked her to the ground. She lay on the ground while he shouted at her. We didn't know if he would hit her again or not. Meanwhile the guy crawling out the window must have been an ally of the woman on the ground because he picked up a loose brick from the ground and began sneaking up on the guy who had hit the woman. When he was close, maybe six feet away he threw the brick and hit the guy who was yelling at the woman, in the back square between the shoulders. The yelling man went down but not hard. The brick thrower turned and ran hardly before the brick hit its mark. The yelling guy recovered pretty quick. He was up before I realized it because the man who threw the brick had jumped the low fence, hit the road and was headed our way. I was watching him jump that fence when Alva said, "Look at the guy who got knocked down."

I redirected my attention to him. He had picked up the same brick that had hit him between the shoulders. I saw him just as he released the brick. He should have been a quarterback. That brick went about thirty yards and directly over the head of the runner. The brick was out of play now. It had been overthrown and went into bushes across the road from the night fighter's house.

The runner came by our car without so much as a word. He was a track star and he was picking up speed as he went by. Almost directly beside us he was met by the guy who was chased by the woman. I had been so busy watching the front end of this show that I had forgot about the two behind us. Somehow, the guy being chased by the woman had managed to get by her and was headed back down the road by our car and toward his house. The two men met, running different directions right beside our car. Neither said a word to the other. The man running from the woman continued on past his house and began to walk as he passed the house. Within a couple minutes, maybe quicker, the large woman who had chased him up the road came walking by. She was winded. We could hear her breathing hard. She was cussing him in between the breaths. We could understand that. We waited and said nothing. They paid us no mind like we didn't exist. We ate some more barbeque sandwiches.

The man who had hit the woman in the back yard stayed in the front yard. Soon the woman came around to where he was but kept her distance. Not much was said. The fat woman went back inside the ram-shackled house. The man who hit the woman in the back yard and the woman he hit seemed to resolve their problem somewhat. They stood closer together and as it got darker, we could see them very well. They went back inside the house together. The last man to run past us, the one who hit the other one with the brick slowly returned to the front yard but never went inside. I never saw the other man return to the scene.

It had gotten nearly dark by this time. Alva kind of laughed and said, "Well, I think it's over. We finished the barbeque. Let's go home."

My Mother said, "I didn't like seeing that. I was sure someone was going to get killed."

Alva turned and said, "Well, it looked like someone might kill the other one there for a while. Irene (the neighbor) told me they do this two or three nights every week. She said that she doesn't see them all day and then they burst out like this about two or three times a week. That's why everyone calls them the 'night fighters'. It is really strange and I believe I have never seen people act this way before. I was hoping they would put on a show for us tonight so that Grant could see how they act. It's really unusual."

My Mother said, "Well, I don't want to see it again. Grant shouldn't be watching stuff like this."

I sat there saying nothing. Silently, I thought, "I've seen worst than this at home."

But, I didn't say a word.

CHAPTER TWENTY FIVE

Trips to Hot Springs

"You always has to have a secret that everybody wants to know." Dewey Smith

While living at the old Brawley School, our most enjoyable times were trips to Hot Springs. Hot Springs was a much more interesting town than Malvern. It was larger and there was more to do. I liked the walks downtown along Central Avenue. Alva had frequented it since he was a small child about 1900. The streets were muddy back then without paving. Gambling and prostitution were common. Alva said he would hold the reins for the horses that pulled the wagon he and his father were driving while his father would go into the saloons to drink. Fights that spilled out of the saloons onto the street were common. He said often two guys would be fighting and the fight would leave the bar and go into the street where they would continue fighting in the mud. Each one knocking the other down until Alva said you could not tell which one was which. Then he said, they would be so tired they couldn't fight anymore. Often they would drag themselves to their feet, go back into the bar and continue drinking. By the time I made my first trip to Hot Springs, the streets were paved and nice. It seemed like a very modern city to me. I had trouble imagining the muddy streets. Of course, I was just a kid. I had seen very little of the world.

Dewey Smith's Town Talk Barbeque was one of my favorites. Alva had patronized his business for years. Dewey made the best barbeque I've ever tasted. His personality came in a close second to the food quality. Many of the local Hot Springs officials came to Dewey's place for dinner. He had a special banquet room set aside for special guests so that they could have the privacy he thought they deserved. We often ate in that area which could accommodate about 50 people. It was his formal dinning room. Dewey did all of his barbequing. He was a master. During our visits he would often take Alva and I into his cooking room where the big broiler was, to show us some special meat he was preparing. He took such pride in it. He was careful to tell me that the secret of his food was his sauce that he made himself.

He said to me once, "I make it and it's my secret. When I die, it dies with me."

Then he'd laugh quietly as he watched my reaction to his comment.

Dewey would continue with sage advice, "Son, you always has to have a secret that everybody wants to know. That makes you stronger than them. When you get your secret, you will be set for life." Then he would chuckle quietly while he watched me digest his suggestion. Dewey was a nice man.

One of our other favorite stops was McClard's Barbeque in South Hot Springs. Cook's ice cream place was a favorite too for their huge milkshakes. My mother loved those. Trips to the Alligator farm and the Ostrich farm were fun. I'd always plead for a trip over West Mountain that provided a view of all of Hot Springs and beyond. There was a nice rest area near the top where the view was terrific. West Mountain was free. It was part of the National Park. A trip up there usually meant we took an improvised picnic lunch. We'd eat and look at the view. So, I got little resistance to my begging for that trip. That was really a lot of fun. There were several restaurants downtown that we frequented. Many of those were along Central Avenue. The Hot Springs Creek ran underneath Central Avenue. When the rains were very heavy, the Hot Springs Creek would exceed it's banks and flood the whole downtown area. I've seen water several feet deep in all the stores along Central Avenue many times. When that happened during a rainstorm, it took weeks for the businesses to clean up and get going again. Following those episodes, there was always a 'storm sale' to get rid of the damaged goods. My Mother loved those because it meant huge discounts.

The gambling and prostitution was still in full swing in Hot Springs when I was a child. I can remember walking by places on Central Avenue and seeing the roulette wheels spinning and slot machines were everywhere. Every bar had its share of slot machines. If we were in a bar, Alva would give me a few nickels and let me play the slots. Imagine a 6 or 7 year old playing the slots without argument from the owners. It happened frequently. Although it was scaled down, it was not too different than Las Vegas is today. Hot Springs was known as "Little Las Vegas". According to Alva, the prostitutes were rampant on the streets. My mother resented that. All I knew was the best dressed ladies I'd ever seen were along Central Avenue. They were in all the doors of the most expensive bars that doubled as gambling establishments. They were friendly too. They would say "Hi" to me. My Mother would get on me for responding to them. She resented me making eye contact with them. I couldn't resist. I was only about six years old but they really looked nice. Now, I'm certain they were going out of their way to attract my attention. They got it.

My Mother said, "They are just doing that in hopes they will get your Dad's attention."

Alva would smile and let the whole thing pass without comment.

Our family had many friends and a few relatives living in and around Hot Springs. We visited with them frequently. That was about the only time I ever played with family. Alva was afraid for me to play with many of the kids in other locations. He was always afraid I'd talk about the whisky business. It made for a rather lonely existence.

CHAPTER TWENTY SIX

Knockout Punch

"The Lord presents us with opportunities sometimes. We must take advantage of those opportunities. If we don't, it's like defying the will of God." Alva Burris

During one of our numerous trips to Hot Springs I saw Alva deliver a single punch to a guy that still amazes me. Alva was about 55 at the time. We always went to the Post Office while we were in town. I believe we had a general delivery mail call at the Post Office. Plus, it was the only place Alva would trust to mail a letter. He mistrusted the small mail drops that were found at random places over town and on street corners. On this particular occasion we had done our normal shopping and bits of entertainment which often included lunch at a favorite restaurant on Central Avenue. We stopped by the Post Office on our way out of town. It was our last stop. Alva parked the car, directly in front of the Post Office building which was quite large. We had all gone in as usual. Alva would dictate what happened inside, but my Mother would do all the letter addressing and purchasing of stamps and things that people do in Post Offices. I tagged along because I wasn't allowed to stay in the car alone when we were in town. Both my parents were concerned about kidnapping and took no risks in that regard.

We had done our business inside the Post Office and had returned to our car parked diagonally at the curb. All of us had reentered the car with me in my typical rear seat position when Alva leaned forward a bit in the seat. He looked intently at two men standing in front of our car. They were talking to each other and were turned with their sides to us.

Alva looked for a moment at them and said, "That's Robert Carter. I haven't seen him in twenty years. I thought he was likely dead. I owe him something from a long time ago. Just a minute."

My Mom said, "Now don't do anything to get us in trouble. Why don't we just go on home?"

She could sense something. She knew the markers when Alva's temper was about to flare. She continued, subtly, to attempt to convince him to forget whatever he was planning. I could see his hackles beginning to rise.

She said again, "Come on, Alva. Leave him alone. Let's go."

Alva said, "Don't worry. I'll only be a minute. I need to say a word to him."

Something about the intensity of his stare and the way he stiffened his body signaled my Mother that a show was about to begin.

Alva got out of the car. He's got my attention now after overhearing my Mother's pleading to get him to forget this 'word' he's about to deliver. When he stepped out, he stood up straight and squared his shoulders. I knew that signal. Something physical was about to happen.

Alva walked quickly up to the two men and touched the one on the left on the shoulder. The man Alva was addressing was slightly taller and he turned slowly clockwise to the right to face Alva. Alva had his back to me but I could see that he was speaking to the man in front of him. The other man backed up a step. He must have heard something that made him move quickly backwards. Something ominous had been said. As the stranger backed away quickly, I saw only what appeared to be the shake of Alva's shoulders. The shake was barely perceptible. I saw no hand or arm movement. To me, it appeared that his hands never left his side. It seemed that only his shoulders slightly shook. I heard the sound of his fist hitting the guy's chin. I never saw the hand/arm movement. The man in front of him that he had been talking to began to fall like when a large tree is cut and begins it's fall. He fell flat on the ground on his back without crumpling or any other movement. Alva squared his shoulders again, looked at the guy on the sidewalk, who was unmoving, turned and stepped quickly back to the car. He got in, started the engine and backed the car out into the street. I could see the guy that he hit still laying on the street, motionless. He was out cold. His arms were spread from his sides and he was as still as he will be when dead. The second man just stood there looking alternately from the guy on the ground to us pulling away in our 1937 LaSalle. I was wondering how Alva hit him without moving his arm. I did not realize that his arm movement was so quick that I had failed to detect it. I was baffled by this seemingly impossible feat for a long time but afraid to ask Alva how he did it. Not until I was much older did I fully realize what I had seen.

My Mother rarely said a word of profanity but she said, "What the hell was that all about? When did you know him?"

Alva said, "I knew him a long time ago when I was married to Violet. He said some really nasty stuff about me and my family. When it happened it was in a place where I couldn't do anything about it. But I told him I'd see him again some day. And that when I saw him, I'd settle the score. Well, today, I reminded him of what he said. I reminded him and then I knocked him on his ass. This is the first time I've seen him since that day. When he wakes up he'll remember that day. And this one too."

Alva said, "That was a score that I doubted that I'd ever get the chance to settle. The Lord presents us with opportunities sometimes. We must take advantage of those opportunities. If you don't, it's like you were defying the will of God."

My Mother just looked at him without saying anything. She shook her head slightly and turned back to face straight ahead. Me? I kept my mouth shut and said nothing. When we arrived at home at the old school house, I was still wondering, how did he do that?

CHAPTER TWENTY SEVEN

Babcock Street

"Someone moved that axe." Lawman at Alva's whisky still

Alva, for a while that we lived in the school house, enlisted the help of Felix, a black man from Hot Springs. Alva brought him out to our 'school house' and let him live in a secondary small building near the school house. He was to help Alva with the heavy lifting required when making whiskey. Felix would stay with us for a few weeks then we would take him back to his family in Hot Springs. This schedule apparently worked well for Alva. During this period Alva traded for a piece of property in Malvern and began building a house on it. He traded the 1937 LaSalle that had pulled the trees from the road after the tornado and some money for the real estate on Babcock Street.

The house in town idea was popular with me. It meant I would no longer have to ride the bus. I literally hated the bus ride. I hated school but the bus ride was what made school so unpopular. With a house in town near school, I'd no longer be required to leave home at daylight and return at dark. The bus ride was tough. I was in the first grade. I was five years old. I was the first person on the bus in the morning and the last one off in the evening. I left our house, the old school house, at 7 AM. Seemed earlier. I returned about 5:30 PM. In the winter it was dark when I left and dark when I returned. I followed this bus routine for the first two years of school. After boarding the bus early and arriving at the school it was necessary to wait on the school ground for about 45 minutes before school began. The reverse was true for the evenings. I had to wait a long time before the bus (called the second bus) delivered me home. The fact that I was younger than everyone resulted in severe intimidation sometimes.

The proposition regarding the real estate in Malvern worked well. Alva completed the house in Malvern to the extent that we could move into it and finished the rest while we lived there. Alva believed that he could leave Felix, the black man, at the school house and have him continue to make whisky. Alva did most of the work and used Felix for carrying heavy objects and for transporting the whiskey in jugs to places away from the still. Alva did all the distillation. This transportation of the whisky to a secondary spot after it was made was an elementary technique of Alva's. He believed, rightfully, that it provided greater security. Things went along well until Alva was nearly caught at the still exactly like his brother, Charlie. Only extreme care and stealth on his part prevented his capture.

As Alva retold the story, I listened. He said he got up early one morning, before daylight, and walked the long distance to the still in his hidden spot in the woods behind the old school house. He was getting prepared to make a run on the still. Alva was a stealthy hunter and probably even more cautious as he approached the still. His memories of his brother Charlie's demise was likely always on his mind as he approached the still. He said daylight was coming as he went over the last hill and began to angle down the mountain to the site of the still. He was a keen observer after years of hunting and watching for animal sign so that he could stalk them better. He was a natural tracker but never considered himself as such. As Alva angled down the hillside he noticed a small twig at a strange angle on a tree alongside the path he was on. The twig was broken. It was broken in a way, as he described, that no animal would have broken it. And, there was no sign of an animal having climbed the tree that had the broken twig. He said he looked at it a long time after he first noticed it. He was reading the broken twig. He was trying to imagine how it broke in the manner it did and what could have done it. After studying it, he said he could only imagine that a human had stood there and nervously broke the twig. He felt a tiny bit of alarm upon this conclusion.

He said, "I was so close to the still and to have a limb broken by a human that close made me believe that the still had been discovered."

He waited a long time at this spot without moving. He said he just melted into a small group of trees that were low on the ground without making a sound. His suburb skill-set from hunting made this possible. He waited, motionless, for a long time. He said, " I think I must have waited for 30 minutes, at least, without making a sound and hardly breathing." At that moment he thought it must have been a false alarm and he had decided to move slowly down to the still site and watch for any additional sign.

Just as he began to move out of his cover, thinking the danger was over but before he had taken hardly a step, he heard someone very nearby say, "Someone moved that ax."

Alva stopped before he had moved an inch. He stopped and remained motionless without making a sound. He said his heart practically stopped beating for a moment.

He said later, "I held my breath because I wanted to listen for any sound. For me to hear a voice, that clearly meant that someone had been standing close by. It meant at least two were within speaking distance."

Whoever had spoken had surely been standing very close without either Alva or the other party knowing the other existed.

Alva said, "My heart was really beating fast now because I didn't know if at any minute someone was going to step out and put a gun on me and maybe kill me."

He said, " I stood there for about 30 seconds or as long as I could hold my breath after I heard the voice then I slowly moved backwards while watching all the woods for anyone to step out."

He said, "I didn't know how many there might be but there was certainly two or more for one to be talking to the other one."

Alva slowly moved backwards one tree at a time keeping a tree between him and the direction the voice came from. One tree at a time he moved back up the hillside until he was at the top. The crest of the hill was about 100 yards from where he heard the voice.

He said, "When I was over the top of the hill, I made my way as fast as I could through the woods and didn't use the path I came on."

The distance was about two miles from our home at the old school house. I remember when he came in. He was out of breath. He looked flustered maybe you could say scared. No doubt he was unnerved. He told my mother about it. I listened.

He said, " I don't think they ever saw me or knew I was there." He said, "But I was so close to being caught. I know exactly how Charlie must have felt just before he was shot."

He just shook his head and had a far away look in his eyes as he tried to get his breath. He knew he had come very close to meeting the same fate as his brother, Charlie. I could see it in his eyes as he finished telling me about it. From that point forward I knew what the expression meant, "One's whole life passed before their eyes". There was no doubt Alva had seen the passage of his life before his eyes.

CHAPTER TWENTY EIGHT

Revenge

He was capable of terrific acts of vengeance if he thought he had been set up by someone

The previously described incident was the topic of many kerosene lamp-lighted late night conversations between Alva and my Mother while we remained in the Brawley School house. She consistently urged him to stop making whisky and let it go. He agreed easily that he would never return to the still sight. However, he wouldn't fully agree to curtail the whisky making. He had been in it so long that it was hard to stop. It is difficult to give up one's craft albeit it illegal. He could not retrieve any of the hardware from the still. That part was certain. He would be forced to abandon everything just as it was, including the "axe" whose movement had saved his life. He did not agree so easily to stop making whisky. Moonshining was in his blood. It was hard to stop.

After many conversations, he seemed to soften a little on the idea of abandoning the whisky making. I remember my Mother's chief argument that seemed most effective. Sometimes, she showed amazing insight into those concepts that made him tick. This was one of those times. I wish there had been more like it.

She said, "This has been a sign from God that you are to stop. He's trying to warn you to stop before you are killed just like your brother."

That seemed to get through to him. He listened to that. Once she saw how effective the statement was, she didn't let up. She had hit a nerve. Mom was like a baying hound once she caught the sent of the trail. She repeated the expression often within her dialogue with Alva although she was not religious or schooled in Biblical history. She knew when she had tapped into a deeply sensitive area. She had scored an infrequent bulls eye with the 'message from God' remark. I could see him ponder it more deeply ever time they would talk about it. He would become silent and think. Alva finally started to give in. He appreciated this "sign" stuff. He believed in such things. I guess it was his Indian heritage that made him depend on "signs". He watched for signs when he planted and signs when he harvested. He sometimes called them warnings. I have a list of events that the decision to do or not do revolved around a "sign" Alva had detected in his environment. He finally started to say quietly that maybe he would just lay low for a while and if he got back into it he would give up making it and just purchase good whisky from someone else who took all the risks. I was small but that sounded good to me. We all knew that the greater risks of Whisky business was those long days at the still when one was distracted by the work at hand and could be apprehended easily. Additionally, I knew we were about to move into town where I would no longer be forced to ride that darn bus. The house was slowly being completed on Babcock Street and I was excited about that.

Alva pondered on his near capture. He could not free his mind of it.

He would say, "There's something about that whole thing that I can't figure out. How did they find the site so easily?"

He would recount how clever he had hid the entire operation. He would speak about how deep in the woods he had placed it and how he never took the same path in so that he would not make a trail.

He said, "That was one of the best places to hide a still that I had found in years."

He would comment, "Only two people knew exactly where that still was. Me and Felix, the black guy."

All of it just made no sense to him. He continued trying to remember any clue that would remind him of something said that related to it. He was capable of terrific acts of vengeance if he thought he had been set up by someone. I was hoping he would forget it all but that wasn't destined to happen. It remained a puzzle to him and he was determined to solve it.

Alva began remembering how Felix who helped him had suddenly told him he was sick and wanted to be taken back to Hot Springs about a week before the incident in the woods at the still. As he recalled it, Felix, who had been living in the school house following our move into town, said he had to get back to Hot Springs in a hurry and wasn't sure if he could come back. Alva had returned him to his mother's house in Hot Springs but found the excuse for leaving quickly a little thin. Alva's temper began to boil again. I could sense that he felt he had been set up. He felt that his helper had ratted on him. My mother tried everything to prevent him from any violence but to no avail. He believed he had put the pieces of the puzzle together. That's when the anger hit him. His face got red and I could see the change. So could my Mother. She knew the danger signals.

Alva said, "I helped that SOB and then he turned on me like this?"

Then he shook his head and got up and walked around the room. My Mother tried to calm him down but it was no use.

CHAPTER TWENTY NINE

Finding Felix

***"I wonder if that guy died"* Gerene Burris**

Alva made a trip to Hot Springs for the sole purpose of talking with his former helper, Felix. I was always along on these trips. About 6 months had elapsed since the close call deep in the woods behind the old school house. Alva had festered for all of those months trying to figure out where he had erred. Alva's conclusion always came back to one item. Whatever had happened, Felix had set it all into motion. When we arrived at Felix's house, he was sitting on the front porch. He recognized us. Alva motioned for him to come to the car. Felix, when approached looked very frightened. It is hard to know if Felix read the look on Alva's face or if it was the guilt gnawing at him. One of those was making him reluctant to get into the car. Alva finally convinced him to get into our car's backseat. I normally sat in the back. On this occasion, my Mother had me sit in the front with her. I sat between her and Alva.

She cautioned me, "No matter what happens, don't you say one word. Do you hear me?"

The way she looked at me set the stage. There would be no backtalk on this subject.

I think, knowing Alva, she believed there would be some violence within the car that she would be unable to control. When Alva was mad, he'd turn on her if she got in the way. Not much different than a mad bull that will charge anything in his field of view.

Barely did I breathe let alone say a single word. Although Alva was quite friendly toward him, Felix either sensed something sinister or he was guilty as sin or both. It was impossible to tell. He was scared out of his wits and could barely talk. Alva picked up on this immediately. My Mother had made Alva promise he wouldn't harm the guy in the car even if he thought he was guilty. Well, no doubt, Alva had tried him and hung him within a few minutes. The poor guy was nearly soiling his pants by just sitting there. After a while, Alva had made his decision. Guilty. He told Felix that their conversation was over and asked him to get out with a promise that he would pick him up in a few days to help him move some whisky still parts to a whole new place. This seemed to console the man and he exited the vehicle. Felix seemed to believe that his act had worked and that Alva suspected nothing. He seemed much more relaxed on exit than on the entry. Of course, I was just a kid but I knew what was going down.

Several days later, I only learned what I knew from hearing snippets of conversation between Alva and my Mother when they thought I was paying no attention. It seems that Alva had gone alone to Hot Springs to pick up Felix at a predetermined time. He picked him up, took him out of town and near the woods where we lived at the school house. Alva took him into the woods and when they were safely away from sight of the road, Alva began to question him. Alva was carrying a 12 gauge double barrel shotgun. Alva threaten to shoot him if he didn't talk. So he started talking. He told Alva many aspects of the sting that Alva did not know. He revealed the period when he lived at the old school house prior to this incident, and while we were away, a game warden had stopped and struck up a conversation with him. The game warden questioned why a black man would move into a school house that was so isolated from town. Finally, the game warden asked him if he was helping Alva make whisky. The black guy apparently became frightened by the white game warden who was wearing a gun. According to Felix's story the game warden was patting his gun frequently to let old Felix know his place. He admitted to the game warden that he was helping make some whisky. The game warden grabbed Felix by the arm, twisted the arm until Felix fell to the ground. Once on the ground with his face in the dirt, the game warden pulled his pistol, placed it behind Felix's ear and threatened to kill him. He made Felix take him to the still sight and show him the operation. Then the game warden returned him to the school house and cautioned him to say nothing about their conversation. He promised to come back and kill Felix if this visit was mentioned. That visit was the motivation for the black man wanting to return to Hot Springs so quickly. That's why Felix suddenly became "sick". Alva said he had planned to probably shoot the guy with the shotgun after hearing the story of how it all transpired and getting the names of who was involved. Alva said that after he listened to the story and realized that the guy had just fell apart in the presence of the game warden he didn't feel like shooting him. He decided to put the gun aside and beat him up. That's what he did. He told my Mother that he leaned the gun against a tree and picked up a rock and beat him until he was unconscious. He said he left him there. In a low voice, she asked if he had killed him.

Alva said, "No, he was still alive. I could see him breathing."

I guess if he had wanted him to die he could have shot him at any time with the shotgun. That is not complete vindication for Alva. However, I got the feeling that he wasn't too concerned if the guy lived or died. He said he left and went to a creek where he washed all the blood off himself and his clothes. I can remember one significant night that he came home strangely wet all over and worn out.

My mother had said, "What have you done?"

Alva said, "Nothing. Keep your mouth shut." With a quick glance at me, he said, in a whisper, "I'll tell you later."

Alva didn't know that I had heard the last statement but I had.

Many times my Mother would say privately to Alva, "I wonder if that guy died."

Alva would answer. "I don't think so. I was by there and I never saw any buzzards circling."

Her questions revealed that she was troubled by the memory of it although she was not directly involved. She wasn't about to put too much pressure on Alva. She knew how far to take the conversation and it never advanced beyond a casual muffled question. It seemed to me, that as time proceeded, Alva was less and less proud of the 'lesson' he had taught Felix. I believe he may have been a bit worried about whether he had killed him or not. It was evident in little snippets of conversation that I was privileged to hear. Alva likely explored the possibility of Felix's demise more than I was aware of at that time. My recollections of events became more clear as I grew older.

CHAPTER THIRTY

Felix Spotted

"Yeah, since it's all over, I guess it's better that he lived over it."
Alva Burris

Some time had passed. Maybe a few months. I'm unsure. I remember Alva returning from Hot Springs. These days, he often went to Hot Springs alone. He seemed anxious to talk to my Mother. That drew my attention although I pretended to be entertained by other things.

He said, "You won't believe who I saw today. It was old Felix. He saw me and he looked really scared. He had some scars on his head and looked like he was healing up. When he saw me he began to run."

My Mother seemed relieved but she was obviously stifling the emotion.

She said, "Are you sure? It could have been someone else."

Alva, with no pretense at masking his relief said, "Oh, I'm sure it was him. He's the tallest guy you will ever see and the only one with his head all cut up with scars. It was him. As soon as he saw me, he put on a look that I will never forget and ducked his head down and started walking. He always had that limp from when someone shot him a long time ago. Remember, I told you about that? And he was limping. No doubt, it was him. It was the same limp. He took a couple steps with that limp of his then he broke into a run."

My Mother, no longer trying to stifle the relief, said, "Well, I'm glad he learned his lesson but didn't die."

Alva said, "Yeah, since it's all over, I guess it's better that he lived over it."

Alva sat for a while with his lips tight and his eyes squinting half closed like he was staring into the sun. If thoughts were round he would have been rolling. I didn't need to be an adult to read the message on his face. Relief was written all over it.

I wasn't supposed to hear any of this. But, I did.

Shortly after this, someone discretely burned the school house and the adjacent building where Felix had lived. Alva learned much later that whoever burned the building thought Felix was still living there. It was burned down at night by pouring kerosene all around each building and setting it on fire. The obvious motive was to kill Felix by trapping him inside. The Klu Klux Klan was secretly strong in this area. In the 1920's they were openly soliciting members. At its peak in the 1920s, the Klan had more than 1,000 members in Malvern and Hot

Springs County, including several ministers of local churches. Local newspapers reported frequently on Klan activities and the papers even printed applications for membership in the Klan. By the time the school house burned in the 1950's they had become secretive, but they still existed and still had their secret nighttime meetings. Alva despised the KKK. He had several disputes with them over the years. Perhaps it was they who staged the bonfire. They were famous for their fires. They called it, "Burnin' 'em out." It was a common way of ridding the community of anyone black or white to whom they took a dislike. Rumors indicated the Game Warden was a member of the local KKK. As I mentioned earlier, they were particularly rough with the black folks. Poor old Felix never knew this happened. He was busy licking his wounds miles away in Hot Springs. But the truth of the matter was, he had dodged the proverbial bullet one more time. In an ironic way, Alva's revenge had nearly killed Felix while saving his life.

KKK FULLY ROBED AND MASKED

Klu Klux Klan Robed for a Secret Night Rally
in Hot Spring County near Malvern Arkansas

CHAPTER THIRTY ONE

Babcock Street

"My Mom waved at me. She thought I was in an airplane." Jeannie Yancy

The Yancy family lived on the north side of us on Babcock St. They had two children. A son named, Richard, who was older than me and a daughter, Jeanie, who was younger. Richard loved baseball. Often, he practiced his pitching with me as his catcher. He had a pretty good curve and a zinger of a fast ball for his age. He told me stories of baseball players and I soaked it up. Sometimes, we'd go out into the open field that was across the road from our house so that we could "pop some flies". That meant Richard would hit the ball high in the air and I'd try to catch it. Richard could hit pretty good. He was a good athlete. I was fast on foot and I'd run down most of his hits. I got so that I'd catch just about anything he hit. It was good practice for each of us and I enjoyed it. We needed more players for a real game. And we needed a smoother surface if we were to hit ground balls. There were none available.

Jeanie and I played some. There was not much common ground for us other than talking and playing games in the dirt between our yards. That was better than nothing but was not very entertaining for either of us. Jeanie was friendly and I enjoyed her company. I'd never had a next door playmate. All this was a big leap for me socially.

Mrs. Yancy was nice. Whenever I'd go to their house, it was always very clean. The floors had linoleum on them. The floors were waxed and I was nearly afraid to walk on the surface for fear I'd mess up the shine. Mrs. Yancy always had some deserts cooked and ready for sampling. I loved that.

Mac, the father, was employed in the mining industry. He was an engineer, I believe. He drove a Studebaker and owned an airplane. They had similar styling. Sometimes he would take Jeannie on a ride in the plane. I think it was a Piper. They would fly over the house. Banked heavily, at about 500 feet, they would wave at us on the ground. This became quite common.

Alva worked steadily on our new house. Once it was built and we moved into it, he was constantly leveling the yard and planting trees and flowers to finish the landscaping. Often Alva would haul dirt from one end of the yard to the other in a wheel barrow. When Jeanie was outdoors she would walk alongside Alva as he hauled the dirt. On the return to get more dirt, Alva would let her ride in the wheel barrow. On one of these return trips, Jeannie's mother backed out of her driveway and passed in front of our house in the Studebaker. Mrs. Yancy waved at

Jeannie as Jeannie went by in the wheel barrow. The wave was returned.

Afterwards, Jeannie turned to Alva and said, "My Mom waved at me. She thought I was in an airplane."

Alva laughed over and over at that comment.

He said, "Jeannie acted like her mother wouldn't know the difference between an airplane and a wheel barrow. I've never heard such a funny expression."

Alva received a lot of enjoyment from Jeannie's comments. She may have reminded him of his life with his two daughters at that age. Life was pretty good for a while. All this was prior to the incident with the game warden.

Alva became involved in growing vegetables and producing milk and butter from the cows we owned. We had two horses. We leased several acres of land a short distance north of our house. Alva planted about 3 acres of it in various crops including several varieties of vegetables, corn, peanuts and both varieties of potatoes, sweet and Irish red skinned. We had chickens and ducks. Each year we would order 100 baby chicks by mail. We raised the chicks. When they were fully grown, we sold most of them and kept about 15 for laying hens. That gave us a stock of eggs for our family and many to sell. Alva managed it all well. We had all the vegetables we could consume plus the surplus that he sold. We had pigs that we raised and butchered for meat and some was sold. We cured our own hams and bacon. It was smoked by Alva in a small building that we had at the rear of our house. That was delicious food. The cows provided more than enough milk and butter for us plus much to sell. We sold the extra eggs that we did not use. Regular customers knew we had these items. They came to the house to buy it with the exception of the vegetables. Alva would drive along some of the streets and sell the vegetables. Our life here must have reminded him of his life with Violet. He had created a self-sufficient cycle again. All he needed was some whisky to sell. That came soon enough.

Alva discussed the whisky issue with my mother. She wanted nothing to do with it again. However, Alva convinced her that he was never going to make it again. He said he would research who made good whisky and buy it from them. That eliminated a huge risk to which he had been subjected previously.

Alva found a seller. I don't know if that man is still alive so I will not give his name. I'll just refer to him as the "seller". Alva made extensive plans with the seller, who was a pleasant person with a farm of his own. He lived near Hot Springs. We visited him and his family many times. He engaged in the manufacture of whisky by having some men he trusted make the whisky at a location remote to his farm. When Alva had made all the preparations with the seller, he began preparations to secure the load once it arrived at our property. The plan was that the driver for the seller would deliver it to a spot on our property where we were farming. Alva picked up the seller and his number 1 hauler. All of us went to the exact spot designated for delivery. Alva directed every movement of the car and how it was to be performed even down to how the vehicle should return to the road. The delivery car could be driven right onto the property and out of site of the road and passersby. Alva proceeded to dig holes in the ground with post hole diggers within the thick pine forest that was on our property. The large five gallon jugs in which the whisky was delivered would be immediately put into these holes in the ground and easily covered by pine needles. Very quickly, large amounts of whisky could be transferred from the car and hidden with no evidence that it was stored underground. All the holes were near a tree so that no one would walk over a hole and fall into it.

When a delivery was scheduled and made, the five gallon jugs were hidden immediately in a location far from where the whisky was buried. Later, usually during the night, Alva would return with an ample supply of one gallon jugs. He would measure the fives up into the one gallon jugs. The one gallon jugs would be hidden again in the holes the appropriate size for them. There were many holes in the ground all over the pine forest. You might be thinking that it would be easy for someone to find and steal. That wasn't the case. No one was allowed on our property. Plus the pine forest was very thick. You could hardly walk through it because the limbs of the trees grew right down to the ground. There was an additional factor too. People who were superstitious would never venture into the pine forest because it was an old abandoned graveyard. There were many stories associated with the forest part of our land. Many of the black folks claimed to have seen ghosts there. Alva helped perpetuate the stories with tales of his own told to any of the delivery people who would listen. Naturally, the stories got bigger as they were told and retold. I never saw a ghost there. But I never went deep in the forest at night. I only went on the outskirts. During the daytime, I've explored deeper into it until I could not walk between the trees. There were several tombstones in there and it was easy to see where time had taken its toll and the graves had caved in.

Alva would make a deal to have someone come pick up a gallon of whisky. He would collect the money in advance. The customer would meet him at a location know as the 'gravel pit'. That was an area that was easily identifiable to most. The customer would come to the door of our home. He would be instructed to go to the gravel pit and wait. Alva would wait a bit. He would make sure the customer wasn't followed. Then he would go by another route to the hiding place, pick up a gallon, deliver it to the meeting place and disappear back into the woods to wait for a clear shot at returning home without observation. This technique worked many times. It was such a polished routine that my mother and I were able to pull it off without Alva's help when he was in jail. I'll get to that later.

CHAPTER THIRTY TWO

Game Warden

"I hated whisky making and everything related to it."

Grant Burris

It would have been nice to wrap up Alva's revenge on old Felix and say it was over, but it wasn't. It was over with Felix but Alva had an axe to grind with the game warden who set it into motion. He was still on Alva's list of people who needed to be taught a lesson in discretion. Alva believed that what Alva did was Alva's business and no one else's business. People who crossed that line must pay a price. The game warden was a daily figure who traversed the back roads and probably thought he had a right to behave as he had. After all, he was a sworn instrument of the law and likely never knew for certain that Alva was the owner of the still he had intimidated Felix into disclosing.

As an aside to the whisky business, we often drove the country roads that passed in front of the old school house. We drove them in search of a deer to shoot for meat. Often they were out of season but Alva felt he had a right to them since they were on land that his family had once owned. He felt like they were a part of his extended herd. And, if he thought we should have some deer meat for the table when there was none of our stock ready for butchering, then he'd simply go drive the country roads, shoot a deer, dress it in the woods. Instant meat for the table. We never wasted any of it.

He'd preface a drive with, "Let's go see if we can see a deer".

Alva believed in consuming all that he shot. He was adamant about this. It was one of his rules.

We were on one of those famous deer drives when we encountered the game warden. Alva carried a seething undercurrent of anger about the game warden's involvement in his close encounter with the police in the woods at the still. Alva believed, deep down, that many of the locals had a vendetta against him. Maybe they did. Maybe they didn't. No matter. I think this was a left over piece of unfulfilled vengeance from emotions he felt when Charlie, his brother, was slain. Alva felt something and needed regularly to break free of the "persecution", whether imagined or real, by kicking someone's ass. Sometimes, it didn't take much to get him fired up. I had witnessed this frequently. The game warden's ticket had been pulled. He just didn't know it yet.

I was in the car in my typical spot, the back seat. My Mother was sitting in the passenger position. We were driving slowly along the dirt road on the way to our home in Malvern and about half way between Malvern and Hot Springs. We were near Cooper Creek where the road splits and one portion goes to Lake Catherine State Park. We passed the game warden who was stopped on the roadside. He was nailing up some paper signs that said, "No Hunting". It was the border line of the game preserve. Alva saw him and it seemed that he went into a different mode. My Mother recognized the change and began telling him to keep driving.

She said, "Don't get yourself into trouble. Keep on driving. Don't stop. Please don't stop."

No amount of pleading made any difference. Alva might as well have been deaf. He was operating on a program for battle. Alva stopped the car, got out and approached the game warden. The game warden was wearing a gun and had a claw hammer in his hand which he had been using to hammer nails into the tree to hold the signs. Alva was unarmed. Alva went right up to his face, snatched the hammer from his hand. Alva hit him with the side of the hammer and the warden went down. Alva continued to hit him and tell him that he had interfered where he had no business. Alva knew that whisky making was illegal. He just didn't think anyone should prevent him from making it. To Alva, this game warden had crossed the invisible line. He had crossed Alva's line. Alva gave him a pretty good whipping and left him on the ground beside the road with the hammer. The warden's gun was still holstered. It happened so quickly. I could barely grasp what was unfolding right in front of me. Alva hurried back to the car with only one glance back at the game warden before jumping into the driver's seat. He likely glanced back to see if the game warden had unholstered the pistol he was carrying.

My Mother was beside herself with frustration. She knew better than to cross him at a time like this but she was repeating over and over, "You damn fool. You have gotten yourself in trouble again." And, she was right again. More than she realized. He was in for a long siege of legal worries this time. She was unaware that this was the beginning of Alva's most challenging legal episode.

I can still remember it happening. It all happened so fast. When he returned to the car he had blood all over him. I thought it was his blood and I was scared, but I quickly realized he was uninjured. The blood was from the hapless game warden.

My Mother, always the one concerned for the victim said, "He wasn't dead when you left was he?"

Alva, out of breath from the fight, said, "No, he was sitting up and mumbling. He wasn't dead."

We raced to town. Alva changed his clothes. He told my Mother to burn those bloody ones and he jumped in the car and told her he would write her, "When I get where I am going."

She yelled, "Where are you going?"

He said, as he backed out of the driveway on Babcock Street, "I don't know yet. Maybe to North Carolina. But don't say anything if they come asking questions."

I watched him spin the tires on the 1954 Chevrolet that he was driving. I thought to myself that I might never see him again.

In a matter of one hour my life had gone from a peaceful drive along a country road to something that was closer to a war zone. All I knew was my dad was gone. We had no car. My Mother was crying and scared. I was crying and scared. The floor had a pile of bloody clothes laying in a heap which my Mother had sworn to dispose of before the police came. If they came. They came.

At least one good positive item emerged from this quagmire. All the people who needed a lesson taught to them had now been "taught a lesson". They had all "got what they deserved." Everyone now realized that they couldn't "abuse Alva Burris". Maybe it was over. The price of teaching them a lesson was running and hiding. My Mother and I paid a price too. I couldn't quite follow the logic. Even at that age, I didn't see a future in my Dad's management style. I resented his methods. I hated whisky making and everything related to it. I resented his absence. I despised all the excuses I had to make to friends regarding his absence. Silently, and deep down inside me, I loathed the whisky business which I blamed for most of the inconveniences that I was experiencing. I just wanted my Dad to have a job like all the other Dads. I could see the link between the problems and the whisky business. At least I thought I could see it. What did I really know about anything really? I was just a kid.

Pretty soon, the letters began coming from North Carolina. One did not require a degree in police science to discover the letters Alva sent contained his letter within a cover letter. They were thick and conspicuous. Inside each one, which seemed to be from a North Carolina relative, was Alva's letter describing where he was and what was happening. He wanted to know what was happening in Arkansas. Had the police asked any questions? Did they suspect him? Yes.. yes. The game warden, of course, had told them exactly who had beaten him up. The police came straight to our house. They questioned my Mother. They questioned me. I had been instructed to say, "I don't know anything." They left me alone for the most part. The police enthusiasm to apprehend Alva was not high. Years later I learned that most of the police cared little for this particular game warden. Most thought the beating could not have happened to a better guy. The fact that he had been beaten with his own hammer while armed with a pistol didn't escape their criticism. At this moment in time, I was worried. I was not worried about the police. The fear of them paled in comparison to what I knew Alva would do to me if I said or did the wrong thing regarding the police questioning. After all, I had experienced multiple times what happened to people who Alva viewed as 'failures to fulfill their obligations'. I was scared stiff of Alva. The police intimidation paled in comparison.

I believe a month or perhaps six weeks passed before the police discovered a lead on Alva's whereabouts in North Carolina. Local North Carolina police went to the house, one of Alva's relatives, and treated him with great respect considering what had happened and the charges against Alva. They told him he was under arrest but they were going to allow him to drive back to Arkansas under his own recognizance. He did that. He completed his return to Arkansas before the letter describing his planned return. He outran the letter. When he returned he had twenty four hours to submit himself to law enforcement. He did as he promised and was soon scheduled to go to trial. Well, he was scheduled. The trail was a long way down the legal road.

Many trips to Hot Springs were required to secure an attorney and to post bail and all the other things required when you beat up a law officer and flee to another state. There, I began my education in law. At least I began the portion of the education that one receives while sequestered in the waiting rooms of various attorneys. I became educated in all magazines. I memorized every wall paper pattern in the waiting room. I was on a first name basis with all the receptionists. I made mental notes of all the seams in the wooden floor. I knew exactly the number of offices in the building. I, especially knew where the toilet was located. I knew how to behave if I was in the toilet and someone came in. I knew how to "get my business done and get out of there." My mother's instructions were ever present. We were always waiting. Waiting. For a while, I believed that the extent of an attorney's duty was to provide a great waiting room. I liked the change of environment but I was bored. Lots of magazines to read. Lots of time in the city with nice lawns and attractive buildings. This wasn't so bad. I was allowed to walk around the streets some. I could walk down the block to the end and back again. That was the rules by which I was to abide. Soon, I began to get acquainted with all the residents along the way. We were in town frequently. Men, home owners, probably retired, were in their yards working on their flowers and doing general gardening. This was Hot Springs. They were likely retirees from the Capone group and others that enjoyed the quiet southern lifestyle in Hot Springs. Who knows? Maybe they were doctors or engineers. They were all friendly. After a while they began asking me questions and I would answer as I saw fit. It would have played differently if I had asked them the questions. The homes were nice with highly manicured lawns. This was a much more affluent neighborhood than I had been accustomed to. It was obvious these folks had money. It seemed unlikely that any of them had ever beaten someone within an inch of their life. Of course, I was just a kid.

CHAPTER THIRTY THREE

The Library

"Always seize the moment" Grant Burris

I remember one particular gentleman who seemed to always be on one knee tending to his flowers in the front flower bed which was adjacent to the sidewalk. He always had a thick towel which he carefully placed on the ground to protect his knee and his trousers. A second towel he always kept folded at his side as he worked. Once, during one of my passes, I noticed the butt of an automatic pistol protruding from the spare towel. The nicely folded thick spare towel was always at his side. I'm sure the pistol was conveniently tucked inside. This man took no chances with whomever he considered to be his enemies. He was always well dressed even when gardening. I'd walk by and he would always look up and recognize me with a smile and a nod. Frequently, he would say, "Good Morning" or "Good Afternoon" depending on which was appropriate. I would smile and say, "Hi". I had been instructed not to become friendly with strangers. However, this man lived here and after numerous salutations could hardly be considered a stranger.

One morning this man got up on his feet as I approached. He waited for me. Something was planned. He was likely about sixty years old and was partially grey. He brushed off his hands as I approached and used that thick towel he always carried to finish the job. After he brushed himself off he dropped the towel and picked up his perpetual spare towel with its mysterious contents. I could tell he was about to address me in some fashion before he said anything. It was obvious he had thought this out and was prepared. As I walked past and our eyes met he said his familiar, "Good Morning." I answered, "Hi".

He paused a moment and something about his demeanor caused me to stop walking and listen. He said, "I've noticed you walking by several times. Do you live near by?"

I answered, "No. I live in Malvern. My parents are busy at the law office." And I pointed to the building which was not far away. He recognized this with a nod and his expression seemed to say that none of this was a surprise to him. His question was more of a salutation than an inquisition.

Then, with a slight twist of his head to punctuate the question, he asked, "Have you ever been to the library across the street?"

Library? I was not aware there was a library across the street. I looked where he pointed and there was a large single story brick building. Sure enough, it said, Library, on the front. I had never noticed because, after all, I was forbidden to cross the street. I think I was forbidden to look across the street without permission. So, things on the other side of the street were another world.

He followed quickly with, "Ask your parents permission and the next time you are up here, I will take you over and introduce you to the people in the Library. It could prove to be enjoyable for you."

Neither of us had any idea just how valuable that visit would ultimately be. That visit would, literally, change my life.

I agreed with his proposal and was excited to have an opportunity to do something I'd never done. I'd never been in a large public library. Doing so seemed like a great idea. It would be the first of my many visits to large libraries and the initiation of my appreciation for information storage.

At the first opportunity upon my return to the law office, I asked my Mother if I could go to the library with this man. She seemed surprised that I had made an acquaintance. She questioned me about him and seemed relieved that he was someone who lived nearby. Of course, she would not make a decision without my Dad's approval. Alva was asked and he said it would be OK if my Mother went with me to meet this man before allowing me to accompany him across the street. Alva seemed more comfortable with the idea than my Mother. I was surprised by that.

During our next visit to the law office, I was anxious to have my mother meet this man and gain permission to cross the street with him. I could hardly get the thoughts out of my mind. I was sure she would approve. I was prepared to negotiate on his and my behalf. I took my first walk down the street and upon seeing him in the yard bent in his usual posture, I returned quickly to the law office before drawing too close to his location. I asked my Mother to come with me to meet him, which she did. They spoke briefly and he explained his idea to have me accompany him to the library so that I could get acquainted with the staff there. He explained that he and his wife used the library a lot since it was so convenient to their home. His explanation and the entire conversation between he and my Mother was a very pleasant thing. I felt relaxed by it and I was anxious to go to the library. He was quite convincing. My negotiation skills were at the ready but they were unneeded.

After my Mother spoke with him briefly she gave her permission. She returned to the law office and I was off to the library with my new friend. Upon entering, I realized the staff knew him well. He introduced me by my name and introduced the staff member whom he had sought out to give me my first tour. This was nice and I was already enjoying myself. I felt respected and I liked the feeling. He waited briefly and the staff member assured him she would watch me and she would accompany me back across the street when I was finished with the tour. This was great.

Her first question was, "What type of books do you like to read."

She might as well have asked me directions to a valley on the Moon. I had no idea how to answer. She saw my puzzled look and smiled. She redirected her question. She said, "What kind of toys do you like playing with the most?"

I answered, " Cars, airplanes and spaceships."

She said, "Well, I know just what you will like. Come with me."

She took me to the Science Fiction area. I've been a fan of Science Fiction since that day. After I looked around for a bit I selected a book which I will never forget. It's name was, "Mrs. Pickerel Goes to Mars". I returned to my courteous assistant and presented her with the book. She told me it was a great choice. She then walked me through the procedure of the card catalogue. She showed me how to find a category and how to find that book number on the library shelf. She said by knowing how to use the catalog I could find any book I wanted if it was in the library. I was proud of my new skill. She said I could check out books, two at a time and return them within two weeks. I was stunned that a stranger would let me take her books home to read. But I was not arguing. I liked this. It would be the beginning of my life-long love of reading. It would be the beginning of countless hours of enjoyment that replaced the would-be boredom. I can never thank that courteous gentleman enough who first introduced me to the Library. I have learned many things that I would not know had he not taken the time to usher me and his spare towel with contents intact, across the street. Although I cannot thank him, I have returned the favor by successfully encouraging all my children, and anyone else who would listen, to read with veracity. I taught them to read subjects they enjoyed first. Then I taught the techniques for reading material rapidly. I believe learning to read well early in life is the cornerstone of all one's knowledge. That can be accomplished by first reading books that are simply interesting. Learn to read rapidly then one can transfer the skills of reading rapidly with retention of information over to consumption of books of greater depth and maturity. The love of reading must be developed first before the skills can be honed to perfection. I have been capable of reading 800 plus words per minute with good comprehension since I was about 10 years old. Before completing high school I was regularly reading at nearly twice that speed. When one is required to read topics for an assignment, it certainly helps to do it at high speed. Later in life, once employed, I benefitted from speed reading when required to read long technical or legal documents. I can't champion good reading skills enough.

Back to the matters at hand. Alva and my Mother made so many trips from Malvern to the attorney's office in Hot Springs that I cannot count them. This continued for about two years, I believe. It started in the summer, lasted through out the following school year and into the next summer. From boring trips that were necessary due to my Dad's behavior, I developed a love for reading that has lasted me throughout my life. With it, I discovered a larger parable. Out of bad things good things can come. One must be ready when opportunities make themselves available. Seize the moment!

CHAPTER THIRTY FOUR

Jail Time

It was like my mother and I were on an island in the middle of the ocean.

During one of those visits to Hot Springs, Alva was scheduled to go to the courthouse which was near the attorney's law office and my mentor who introduced me to the library. I'm unsure what had been scheduled for that morning that Alva went to the Courthouse with my Mother and me in tow. I believe he must have been under bail during all those attorney visits. The attorney had been continuing the case many, many times with the strategy in mind that the older the case became the less likely the court would pursue it with aggression. If my memory serves me correctly, Alva had experienced a preliminary trial and had been found guilty. Following conviction, he had appealed the decision. During all my walking summers where I had enjoyed the library and reading, Alva had paid the attorney to ask and receive continuances. That had been successful in securing his freedom until this particular morning. On this morning, Alva was asked to report to the Courthouse. Upon his arrival, and as quickly as they confirmed his identity, he was taken into custody and placed into jail. I was so surprised. Alva seemed a bit nervous but not terribly surprised. He likely knew more than this naive kid who stared wide eyed at all the uniformed police in their station at the Courthouse.

We were in the sheriff's office for Garland County.

Alva allowed them to lead him from the room and as he rounded the corner before beginning his accent to the jail one floor above the room we were in, he turned and looked at me and waved good bye. There was a pause and long look directly at me as a deputy had each of his arms. The deputies were not forceful or aggressive. They were just doing their routine job as escorts. Alva paused, gave his lips a lick with his tongue, flashed a smile and as he waved he mouthed the word, "Goodbye".

ALVA AS HE APPEARED ON THE DAY HE WENT TO JAIL

My emotions overwhelmed me as I grasped the enorminity of the situation, finally. I began to cry. It wasn't enough anyone would notice but the tears began to roll down my face as I finally understood what he had been trying to avoid. And as I finally put the pieces of this long drawn out scenario together, I realized Alva was going to jail for the crime he committed. I connected the two events. He was going to jail for beating up the game warden. I didn't know what would happen to him and I wasn't sure if I'd ever see him again. My mother, when I glanced up at her, was crying too. She put her arm around me and I put mine around her as we stood in the middle of the sheriff's office. The room was filled with uniformed deputies. Some were manning radios behind a long desk. Others were just milling around the large room being deputies. It was like my mother and I were on an island in the middle of the ocean. The world was going by but there we were, stranded on our island, alone. A woman and a kid oblivious to the world just standing there crying and hugging each other.

I can hardly recall any of our trip home that day. My Mother drove. She kept saying, "We will just act like Alva is still living with us. We won't tell anyone that he's in jail. Don't tell anyone at school. If anyone asks, we will just tell them he's on a trip."

That sounded pretty good to me. I hadn't thought about that aspect of it but it made some sense. I was glad Mom had thought of this possibility. My Mother was afraid that someone might take advantage of the situation if they knew we were alone. While I was afraid of Alva's temper, I secretly relied on his protection. For I knew everyone else was frightened of him as well.

We lived on Babcock Street in Malvern, Arkansas. My dad had a lucrative whiskey business going prior to his apprehension. The customer base was developed and no new sales were needed. We had a generous supply of cash to see us through. Alva had ample amounts of whiskey measured into gallon jugs and hidden well. My Mother knew all the hiding places. It was buried in the ground in individual holes by the pine trees. There were a lot of pine trees on our property. Property that Alva, once more, was farming and growing vegetables upon. We had two milk cows and some chickens and ducks. Mom managed all the animals and crops single handed while Alva was away. I helped her. It was fall and most of the crops were done for the year. The animals required plenty of work. The cows required milking every morning and every evening. During the day, and before school, I would take the cows from our house on Babcock back to the pasture for day of grazing on the grass. In the evening, after school, I would go get them from the pasture, bring them the short distance to our house by leading them on a rope that I placed over their horns. When the cows reached the house, they were fed and while they ate, in a small fenced area, my Mother milked them. When finished we would release the cows in the small fenced area of our yard and they would spend the night there while waiting to be returned to the pasture the next morning. Since I had to leave early for school, my Mother would frequently take the cows to pasture. This routine was already established before Alva went to jail. No modification was needed due to his absence.

In regards to the whisky, that was a new experience. Mom made the decision that she would sell some of the already prepared and hidden whisky. She decided when that supply was gone, she would purchase no more regardless of how many people wanted to buy. That suited me fine.

"However," she said, "We need to make some money and as long as that's already there, I think we can safely sell what we have then forget it after that."

Mom considered this for a minute, then said, "We will just sell what Alva already has hidden and sell it to regular customers and then we won't buy any more."

I said, "OK Mom."

She said, "We will have to be really careful. We cannot let the customers know that Alva is gone. If they knew he was gone, they might try to take advantage of us. We will just tell them where to go wait since they already know where to wait. I will just say, Wait in the same place and Alva will bring it to you like always."

She said, "That way they will think Alva is delivering it to the spot. Then you and I will go down there in the dark. You will take the pistol. You will stand near the spot where Alva always delivers it but stay back in the dark with the flashlight. They won't know you are there. You can protect me if someone tries to get me or tries to steal the whisky."

Mom was staring just past me without making eye contact. I know my Mom was scared of the whisky customers. She was planning her strategy on the fly. She wasn't asking my opinion. She was throwing it against the wall to see if it stuck. It sounded pretty good to me. I liked the part I would play with the pistol. I liked the role of protecting my Mom. I accepted the possibility that I might be required to shoot someone while in that role. I gave no thought to what might happen to me afterwards. After all, I was just a kid.

She said, "I'll go get the whiskey. I'll bring it and say to him, Alva was doing something and sent me to give it to you."

Then she looked at me and said, "Don't let them get me. OK?"

I said, "I won't, Mom. I will watch and I won't let anybody hurt you. I promise."

I meant it. I was serious. I was dead serious. I was only 10 but I shot well. Mom knew this. She had seen me hit the heads of nails, repeatedly, at 25 - 30 feet (One of Alva's tests) with that same Colt 38 Super that I would be carrying. Mom trusted me to protect her. Otherwise, I think she would never have undertaken such a brazen maneuver.

During the first sale, I was a bit nervous. Maybe more than a bit. After that, I didn't shake as much. I'd watch from a few feet away from where the transaction would take place. I'd position myself ahead of time. On this first night, we took a short cut to the place where the whiskey was hidden. We walked normally until we were past the three houses that separated us from the field. Once past the houses and inside the field fence, Mom and I ran through the open area. I split off from her path to go to my assigned spot. I walked carefully the last few steps to make no noise. I waited there and listened for Mom to come with the whisky. After the short run she would break back to a walk and go through the pines to the hiding place. The pines were thick and it was impossible to run while in the thick stand of trees. One was required to walk even during daylight. Plus, this stand of trees contained several old graves. It was easy to step in one of those in the dark. I don't know what happens when one steps in a grave at night. I don't want to know. Once she had the jug of whisky from it's hiding place from one of the many holes Alva had dug, she would walk carefully, so as not to fall and break the jug, and arrive slightly after me at the assigned spot. All this only took a few minutes. It could be accomplished by the time the customer had walked from our house to the designated spot. His path was slightly longer than ours. We were meeting near the gravel pit.

Just as she started to approach the customer, who was always a black man and often a large black man, she would flash her light once as she had told him she would. The single flash of the light was the predetermined signal. He was instructed to cough twice in response to the flash. That would let her know she was approaching safely.

She had instructed the customer, "When you see my light flash, just cough twice so that I will know it's you. You'll be waiting right by the fence and I'll just walk right up to you. Don't you move until I get to you."

When I saw that light flash, I didn't wait for trouble to happen. I was in the dark and no one knew I was only a few feet away waiting quietly. I was trying to breath quietly although I was out of breath. I raised the flashlight with my left hand and lifted that 38 Super with my right hand. It was a little heavy for me but I had found a small limb to rest my right arm upon. It was cocked and locked and my thumb was on the safety. My left thumb was on the flashlight switch. I was ready with both thumbs. My plan was to click the safety on the pistol and the switch on the flashlight at the same time, if I was needed. I had practiced this move with an empty gun many times. My plan was if my help was needed, as soon as the guy was lit, I would shoot. I had gone over it in my mind. I was confident that I could shoot accurately without fear of hitting my Mother. We had discussed how she would stand well to the side of my sight line so there was less chance of being hit if I had to shoot.

My Mother flashed her light. The customer coughed twice. My Mother must have been nervous. She had to be although it didn't show. I raised the flashlight with my left hand, thumb on the switch. At the same time I raised the pistol with my right hand. My right thumb was on the safety ready to click it down to the fire position if necessary. Surprisingly, my hands were steady as I tried to make out the figures in the dark. To me, it was just a target that I might be required to shoot, accurately. Mom's coat was long and light grey. I could see her easily. There was just a little moonlight. I think I didn't need the flashlight. Mom approached the customer. He looked even larger in the dark. He was just a silhouette. I knew I couldn't hold this position long but all this shouldn't take long. I never knew his name as was often the case. I rarely knew their name and if I did, it was only their first name. Since she had taken the money in advance at the house, she simply handed the jug, wrapped in a gunny sack, to him.

He said, "Is that you Ms. Burris?"

She said, "Yeah, Alva just handed me the jug and told me to bring it on over to you. He knew who you were and trusted you to act right."

He said, "Oh, yes Ma'am. I always liked Mr. Burris. He's helped me many, many times. He can trust me. He knows that."

Mom said, perhaps regaining some of her confidence, "Well, that's good. Alva said that too. Now, you get going before somebody pulls in here with their lights on and gets suspicious."

He said, "Yes, Ma'am. Yes, Ma'am. That I'm doing. Thank you. I'll be real careful on the way back."

As he walked away, I lowered the 38 Super and not a moment too soon. My arm was hurting from the shoulder down from the weight of the gun. I could feel the ache in my forearm for I had been squeezing the stock of that pistol, without realizing it, with all my strength. I was thinking, next time, if there is one, I hope they don't talk so long.

Mom waited a long minute in the dark. The customer was gone. Then, in a low voice, she turned and said, "Grant?"

I answered and stepped from the bush cover where I was and walked to her. It was only a few feet.

She said, "Where were you?"

I gestured behind me, and said, "Right there behind that bush."

She said, "I didn't know where you were but I knew you were close. I could just feel it. I wonder if he knew you were there?"

I said, "I don't think he knew. He didn't act like he saw me."

"Yeah. He didn't act like it."

We just stood there in the dark for a minute. Thinking. Trying to think of all we had just accomplished.

Mom was having trouble thinking of something appropriate to say. She wanted to fill the silence but didn't know what she should say.

She said, "Does your flashlight work OK?"

I said, "Yeah." And I flashed it on briefly to prove it. Another long pause. Mom was letting it all soak in.

Mom said, "Well, we did it. Let's go back home."

I said, "OK, Mom."

Mom was returning to her natural state and could not pass up a chance to give some motherly advice which likely made her feel more in control.

She looked at me in the dark. Then she said, "You be careful with that gun. You hear me?"

"OK, Mom."

I was proud of her trust but I was especially happy that it wasn't necessary to use the gun. All I needed now was a way to get that adrenalin out of my system since it would not be needed tonight.

My steps along the path were much longer on the way back. Way longer. At least it seemed so to me. I am also certain that my height was slightly greater than when I left the house only minutes earlier on my way down to the field. At least that is the way it felt that night in the woods in Arkansas. Of course, back then, I was just a kid.

The preceding was a recipe for many trips we would make into the pine woods to deliver a gallon of whisky. We used the same routine and not once did we have a problem with a customer. Maybe it was good planning. Maybe it was luck. At least it's over.

CHAPTER THIRTY FIVE

Jail Time

Alva was happy to have the fresh breakfast

GARLAND COUNTY COURT HOUSE IN HOT SPRINGS ARKANSAS

I'll always remember the ring of the steel as those heavy jail doors shut. The sound of the heavy lock going over center and fastening the door shut is still as fresh as the first time I heard it. There was a permanence to the harmonics in that sound that made anyone glad to be on the free side of the door.

Mom and I were relaxed at our house although Alva's absence left a noticeable void. Alva filled a large part of the emotional real estate when he was there. It was his nature. Mom waited until Saturday before going to Hot Springs for the first visit to the jail. I had never been to a jail. The idea was something that I could not get my mind around. She said she had been to a jail once before to visit someone. She said it frightened her to go to a jail. Naturally, it frightened me. If she harbored those feelings, they easily transferred to me.

I didn't know what to expect. We left early on Saturday morning. Mom talked all the way as we drove to Hot Springs. She was nervous about what to say and do. She didn't know what her new responsibilities were. She didn't know what Alva would expect of her. As it turned out, Alva was much less demanding than she expected. She had gotten up early, cooked a nice breakfast. We ate and she prepared a full meal for Alva.

She said, "We will take this to your daddy because I don't know if they feed them enough in jail. I've heard they nearly starve them. So we will take this to make sure he has enough food."

As I said, Mom talked all the way. She was nervous. I think she was listening to herself. She needed to run a few ideas past herself and see how it sounded. I just listened without a word although once in a while she would glance at me and say, "Are you listening to what I'm telling you?"

I would say, "Yes, Mom."

She would continue. Some was repetitious. I understood what she was doing. She was rehearsing what she would tell Alva. Although he was jailed, he still exerted a strong influence. She didn't want him mad at her. She had a deep fear of Alva. So did I, but not as much so as my Mother. That's because I was dumber than my Mother.

We arrived at the courthouse with it's jail on the top floor. Actually, the men's jail was on the top floor. The ladies jail was on the ground floor. Alva told me once there were more crimes committed within the jail than on the outside. It may have been true. We were required to wait when we arrived. We waited until a deputy could escort us up the stairs to the men's area. There was a thick metal door that first must be entered to get into the jail area from the sheriff's office. That door was a real jail door. It was just like the one we have all seen in the movies. Large bars held together by even larger straps of steel. It said "Jail" and "Security" all over it. No one needed to tell you that it was the door of the jail. It made a loud clang when it was shut. After that, there was another solid metal door with a vent screen on the upper half that required unlocking before one could travel up the stairway to the upper floor and ultimately to the men's area. Once we were up the stairs, we could see the entire cell block. It was large. Within it were individual cells with metal bars that could be locked separately within the main cell block. There were cots all around the perimeter of the cell block. Cots were inside the individual cells also. I could see about 30 people milling around involved in various activities. Each in their turn gave us long furtive looks. Almost immediately I saw my dad. He was the only one with no hair. He was a few feet away from the cell block wall and was probably watching for us. He walked over immediately. He was glad to see us and smiled and said 'hi' to me right away. He had on a big smile.

The deputy said, "Well, it looks like you found who you came for. Excuse me. Visit as long as you want. If you need me I'll be downstairs. If you have an emergency, push that red button on the wall."

I believe there was a button on the wall that a visitor could press for emergency assistance if needed. It's the one the deputy had referred to. It was connected to a bell in the deputy's office downstairs. It could only be reached only by visitors and not by the inmates. Alva and my Mother talked and they both seemed happy to see each other. Alva had made a short list of some things he needed. It was things for personal hygiene and it also included a request for his knife. He said he was not supposed to have a knife. So, he would be required to keep it secret. He wanted some form of protection if someone were to attack him. My Mom agreed to fill his request on the next visit. Alva was happy to have the fresh breakfast. He kept thanking my Mother. He quickly said he wanted to share it while it was hot with an acquaintance he had made in confinement. I was overwhelmed at the level of affection Alva showed her. It was unusual. I couldn't get over the absence of furniture and the stark presence of everything made from steel or concrete. The echoes were overwhelming. Each loud sound bounced off the walls and became a sound different than it's origin. Each slam of a steel door was like a rifle shot. It was like nothing I had experienced before. It was more severe than being in a cave by far. It took a long time to adjust to the new sounds and even longer to adjust to the idea of my dad being locked in such a place. I was wondering what I would tell anyone at my school if they should ask. I decided quickly that I was going to tell no one. I kept that promise to myself although Alva never asked me to do so. I kept that promise for the six months he was incarcerated.

CHAPTER THIRTY SIX

Jail Visitations

The echo effect was tremendous

During the time that Alva was in jail meant that my Mother and I went to Hot Springs every week end. She also went every other day during the week too. All my week ends, at least on Saturday, were consumed by the trip up there and back. The time spent at the jail was boring beyond belief. I was desperate for something to do. If I had a book from the library, I'd read it but there was no comfortable place to sit. My Mother and my Dad were worried about me. It may have been a place with lots of locks and keys but it was not necessarily safe.

On more than one visit I asked if I could go down and see the women's jail on the bottom floor. It was just something different to do. Alva always knew if there were any women in the lower portion of the jail. There were never many occasions when women were locked up downstairs. He said that sometimes the women, when they were downstairs and not locked in a cell, would come upstairs at night to make contact with the male inmates. They could not get in but they could visit through the bars and screen like we did. When they were caught, they were herded back to their area downstairs. The deputies didn't like for them to be up with the men. Alva said the some of the women were nice and talked normal. Others were local prostitutes and would do anything the men asked if they had the opportunity even through the bars. Usually they were caught before anything could transpire but it wasn't for lack of trying.

When no women were downstairs, I'd often go down there and explore. It was a large area. It had about thirty individual cells and a central area too. It was the same size as the men's jail. Sometimes I'd sit down there and read in one of the cells. Sometimes, I'd shut one of the cell doors and pretend I was in jail. Once was enough. That was not fun. It was very depressing. Sound carried so well through out the jail that I could hear and understand nearly every word that my Mother was saying upstairs as she visited with my Dad. The echo effect was tremendous. That added to the starkness of the place. The sound effects were better than those created for creepy movies. I certainly never want to be in jail for any reason.

CHAPTER THIRTY SEVEN

Inside the Jail

"I want you to promise me that you will never do anything that causes you to be put into a place like this." Alva Burris

During a couple of the visits my dad asked the jailer if we, my mother and I, could be allowed to come into the jail with him. It was allowed. The reason was that on certain Sundays the local church would enter the jail area and hold a improvised church service within the jail. The purpose, I suppose, was to save the souls of those inmates who would go to hell without their help. I was allowed to experience this from close up. The church happened to be Pentecostal. They are known for talking in "tongues". I'd never experienced this before. It was an experience not easily forgotten. Not only do the members speak in some alien sounding language, they fall onto the floor and writhe around like they had fallen insane. My dad warned me that was about to happen during the service. I thought surely he was just trying to add to the jail experience. Soon, he was proven correct. First one, then another church member would begin talking with words that could not be understood by me or, apparently, by anyone of their other members. Their eyes would slowly begin to roll up into their head. Then they would fall onto the concrete floor and continue to make noises that was later explained again as "speaking in tongues". If I live to be a thousand, I will not understand this. It was a real show although a bit frightening to me. At first I thought they were faking a performance. As the "service" continued I realized that they were in the power of something and likely were not faking their performance. In fact, when one or another of them would recover they would lie there momentarily as though they were regaining their senses, then they would get up one by one and sit on the steel bench again without making eye contact with either us or their church members. It seemed to take a bit for them to fully recover and resume their attention of what was happening. It was a strange happening to say the least. I was happy to realize that they were all locked within steel bars in case they protracted their experience beyond the thrashing on the floor episode. My dad would poke me in the ribs and nod toward one when they were about to go into their act. It was an unusual experience. I felt a strange combination of fear, embarrassment and amusement.

When the church 'service' was complete and the holy rollers had left, my Mother and I had a chance to just sit with my dad and talk for a while. It was a welcome relief from the church folks. Alva always seemed to enjoy those time periods. He would ask for all the smallest details of what was happening outside. My Mother would take her time explaining it. Alva seemed to appreciate it deeply. I had not known him to behave so well except under these unusual circumstances. Once when we were visiting him, as I've described, he asked for my attention for a moment.

He looked me in the eyes and without blinking once he said, "Grant, I want you to promise me that you will never do anything that causes you to be put into a place like this."

I understood what he meant. I nodded and said I would promise.

He said, "I want you to look around at the people in here. Their lives are wasted. And they are responsible for wasting their lives. So, promise me that you will not waste your life. It's all before you. Make something of yourself and stay away from people who have been in jail. Any time you spend in a place like this is wasted time and could easily result in you loosing your life to someone who is locked in here. All of them have weapons that they have sneaked in by some means. Some are pretty nice to talk to sometimes if you have no one else to talk to. However, many of them would kill you in a heartbeat if they thought you had something they wanted or needed. They prey on the weak or the ones they think are weak. Never get yourself into a place like this. Promise me that right now."

I looked directly into his eyes and I said, "I promise".

Little did he know that I was only repeating something that I had already promised myself. Still, it felt good to hear his advice. I've followed it the rest of my life and have avoided jail. I kept my promise.

1615 Babcock Street, Malvern, Arkansas

My home on Babcock Street was simple. It had two bedrooms, a kitchen and a living room with an outdoor toliet. The outdoor toilet was not too uncommon at that time. Only about 50% of the people had indoor plumbing. The house was more attractive when we lived there. This photo was taken by me approximately 2011.

CHAPTER THIRTY EIGHT

Alva Returns from Jail

"It looks like you would respect Grant and let him get some sleep." Gerene Burris

It seemed like from the moment Alva returned from jail he had a vendetta on my Mom. I'll never know why. He accused her of being unfaithful to him while he was in jail. Truth is, if she had wanted to be unfaithful, I think she would not have had time. From daylight until dark and long after dark she was busy with the animals. She milked the cows. We had two. She fed everything, with my help, of course. We ferried the cows to a pen in our yard each evening so they could be milked. In the morning, we took them to the pasture for the day. There were a few vegetables to be picked. There was whisky to be sold at night. It was endless. In addition, every other day my Mother went to Hot Springs and visited with Alva. If Mom was unfaithful, then she had her work cut out for her. She was busy always with the chores and seemingly never a free minute. In addition, how would he know if he was in jail?

However, when Alva returned from his six months in jail, right away he began accusing her of being less than faithful. I think he was paranoid. The arguments escalated. Many times they would wake me in the middle of the night arguing. Alva always won the argument because he ended it with hitting her until she shut up. I can still remember the screaming in the middle of the night. I would listen for a bit then when the screaming and hitting started I'd get up and go into the door of the room. I'd yell his name, afraid to get close.

He'd stop and reconcile himself and say, "Get to hell out of here."

It was enough to shake him back into his senses I suppose. It usually seemed to end after that. Sometimes, my Mother, with a battered lip would come into my bedroom and ask if she could sleep the rest of the night in there. I always said yes. Sometimes I'd hear her crying for a long time. Other times, Alva would follow her in there and continue cussing her.

She would say, "It looks like you would respect Grant and let him get some sleep even if you hate me. He has to go to school tomorrow."

That would often work and he'd go back to bed. Of course, it was difficult to sleep after that.

CHAPTER THIRTY NINE

Alva Teaches me Business

We opened the box lid and looked down into a square cluster of yellow chicks. They were wall to wall.

Alva had his faults but among them was not his business practices. He knew how to make a profit from his work and he attempted to teach me the process. He wanted to illustrate the rewards of good business practices. One of those I remember well is the art of raising chickens and selling them. He made a great example of this.

He said to me one day, "Grant, how would you like to raise some baby chickens and sell them to make some money?"

I answered, "Sure. I'd like to do that. How do you do it?"

He said, "Well, it's easy. I've done it before and it's profitable. We will order 100 baby chicks from a place that sells them. I have the address in a catalog. Gerene can help us. When they arrive, you will have to help with feeding and watering them everyday. It's real important to keep enough food in their trays so they don't go hungry. If they get hungry, they will start pecking each other. Then some of them will die and that costs you money. So, you have to promise to keep them fed. Can you do that?"

I said, "Yes, I can feed them. It will be fun."

He said, "After they grow up and become ready to sell, we will take them to some of the same people we know and sell them. We can take about 10 at a time in the wooden cage we have. When we get back home we will count our money and write the numbers in the book we will keep. In that book we will keep a record of all the money we spend for feed. When the last one is sold, we will total up the money that we made from selling them, subtract the cost of the feed and the original cost of the chicks when we ordered them. The difference between those two numbers is how much profit we made. I will loan you the money to buy the chickens. You can pay me back when we sell all of them and tally up your profit. Does that sound like fun?"

I thought it sounded way too easy. I liked it better than selling whisky. I said, "I will be glad to do that. When can we order the chicks?"

I'd never heard of ordering chickens by mail. Could that even be done? Order live chickens in a box? Apparently, it was common for Alva. He had done it before. He talked to my Mom and had her look up the name of the supplier in the farm catalog. Mom wrote a letter telling them what we wanted after she found all the details in the catalog that we received regularly. Mom gathered all the chicken details, prices and shipping cost. Then we went down to the post office and purchased a money order. We had no checking account. We dealt in cash only with the whisky. The whisky customers all demanded cash transactions anyway, not many people wrote checks for purchases in that time period in Arkansas. Certainly no one wrote a check for moonshine whisky.

Alva said, "It's important for Grant to know that even though we use cash all the time, we can't send cash in the mail because it might be stolen. Sometimes people rob the mail if they think cash is in the envelope. So never put cash in a letter."

We put the money order in the envelope with the letter detailing what we wanted exactly. Mom was good at things like this. Alva was happy. He continued with little snippets of advice regarding this endeavor.

He said, "Gerene, how long do you think it will take to get those chicks?"

Mom said, "Well, the supply house is in St. Louis, Missouri. They rush the order when the items are alive like these chickens will be. So, I think we will get them in about 10 days."

Alva said, "Well, we'd better get busy when we get home and get a place ready for them to live. We will make a little chicken house that we can shut the door on. The first house for them will be small and on four legs off the ground so we can put a light bulb in it to keep them warm easily. After they grow I little bit, we will build a little house with some poles in it to roost on. We will make a little pen on one side of that house for them to spend the day in. At night, they will roost in their house. We will shut the door at night so that nothing can get in and catch them. In the morning, early, you can let them out for the day before you go to school. That will be your job. That and feeding them when you are home. One feeding in the morning and one feeing in the evening. Always keep plenty of water in their water bowl. Pretty soon, they will grow up and we can begin selling them to customers."

About ten days, exactly, a box arrived by mail. The postman delivered them in his car. He carried the box right up to the door and knocked. He could barely carry the box. It was about one foot high and four feet on each of the other sides. I could hear a high pitched chirping inside. There were little holes in the sides and occasionally a little yellow head would peak out the hole. It was, I think, one of the most pleasant experiences I'd had. Those little chicks were chirping their heads off in that box. It was such a pleasant sound. They were such helpless infants. Everyone, including the postman was smiling. Mom was busy getting a place cleared out on the floor where we could set them temporarily. The postman came in carefully and sat them down. She asked if we owed any more and he declined.

He said, "It's all paid for. You're ready to go."

I wanted to open the box immediately and look but Mom made me wait until Alva returned from where ever he had gone. I think he may have been down in the field hiding some whisky. Shortly, he returned and immediately I asked if we could look at the chicks. He was almost as excited as I was. We opened the box lid and looked down into a square cluster of yellow chicks. They were wall to wall.

I was surprised. I said, "I thought you said they were white chickens."

Alva laughed and said, "They are white. All little baby chickens are yellow when they first hatch. These are called day old chicks. They hatched the day before they were shipped to us."

I noticed quickly that two were not moving. They were lying on their side and others were running over them. I asked why they were dead.

Alva said, "Well, there's only two dead. That's pretty good. Sometimes there are more depending on how roughly they were handled. Some will always be dead on arrival in a case like this. But two is not bad. We will get them out into their cage so they will have more room. Then no more will have to die."

We took them out to their four legged cage which was three times the size of the box. Alva had me take them out carefully one by one and set them into their cage. I did it too slowly so Mom helped me. Alva wanted me to have the experience of handling them and to learn what it was like. That was a good experience. Alva was very considerate with animals and chickens. He may have abused my Mom but he never abused animals and livestock of any kind.

We filled their troughs with chicken food. We filled their water dishes with water. The water dish was a one gallon pickle jar with at big mouth filled with water quickly turned upside down in a heavy dish like a pie pan. A small stick was tucked under one side to allow the water to come out. It became an automatic watering system. I had not seen this done. I thought it was clever.

We had chickens and I couldn't take my eyes off them. Mom rigged up a light bulb and gathered some old army blankets to cover the top so that at night I could let the blankets down over the sides to keep them warm. I believe we only left one side exposed during the day. I was in the chicken business.

The chickens grew as Alva had described. When they were ready for sale, we drove through the black neighborhoods where we knew many families. We would take about ten adult chickens on each trip. It was easy to sell them. Alva and my Mother did the selling. I only watched. The families were happy to purchase them from us. Often they would ask us to bring them additional chickens. Once our chickens were ready to sell, we sold all that we planned to sell in about two weeks. We kept the 'pullets', the female chickens that my Mother thought would be good 'layers', or good hens to lay eggs. From those last remaining hens, we had more than enough eggs for more than a year.

Alva's example was a good one. Although they were considered my chickens, I did much of the work of feeding them and cleaning the cages while Mom and Alva did the majority of the real work. I learned a great deal from this example. Alva is to be complimented highly for teaching this.

CHAPTER FORTY

Truck Windshield

I didn't see the pistol in the truck driver's hand.

The nature of our work caused us to frequently drive through the less developed parts of town. On one of these trips along the edge of town that took us across the Missouri Pacific Railroad, through a wooded area and across a large creek with a bridge that had no guard rails, we happened to pass a parked log truck. It was a specific type of log truck familiar to that area. It was called a pulpwood truck. The small pine trees that it hauled were cut short and stacked sideways or perpendicular with the center line of the truck. It was a common method of hauling this type of timber to the pulpwood mills where paper products were made from the pulp of the wood.

As our car passed the old Ford pulpwood truck that was parked alongside the road I noticed two occupants in the truck. Two hillbilly types were sitting in the cab. They were probably drinking some whisky. It was not an unusual scene.

Alva recognized the driver. It was someone to whom he owed a 'lesson'. Alva paused alongside the truck, opened his door and talked over the top of our car to the driver. He let go with a mouthful of profanity directed at the driver of the truck. I was confused by his references to a previous event. In normal fashion, my Mother began immediately to try to calm Alva down. Her cautions were of no use. It was never worthwhile to try to calm him down. He could not be calmed once the cork of his emotional bottle had been removed.

Alva made several comments to the driver. I can't remember the nature of them but it pertained to something the driver had done earlier in life. After the comments and threats had been exchanged, and the threats were exchanged from each person, Alva jumped back into our car and floored the Chevy we were driving. Our tires spun as we crossed the one-lane wooden bridge. I liked that. The thrill of the tire spin temporarily made me forget what might be about to happen. I forgot that each had threatened to kill the other. I didn't see the pistol in the truck driver's hand. Alva seemed to be trying to get away. I assumed it was to save his and our lives. I liked that part also.

Our race to get away was short. Alva was trying to put some distance between us and the driver of the truck. He wanted to get out of pistol range. My Mother, as usual, was making all her customary pleas to persuade Alva to continue ahead. He would hear none of it. Instead, he reminded her that the guy had pulled a pistol and was beginning to aim it at her side of the car. We pulled to the side of the road. We are now in front of a row of houses. Farther up the road and on our left was Wilson High School. Wilson was a school for black kids at that time. On this trip we had a model 94 30-30 Winchester rifle in the back seat. Our guns were always loaded. I was partially sitting on it. If I sat in the back, I was always sitting on a gun.

The instant that Alva stopped, he jumped from his front seat and opened my back door, wide. He yelled for me to get down and grabbed the Winchester from under me. My window in the back door was down because it was a hot day. When Alva grabbed the rifle, he cocked the hammer as he pulled it out. He moved back ahead of my open back door, placed the rifle across the window opening, yelled at me to stop moving around (I was shaking the car) and put a bullet through the driver's side windshield of that old Ford truck.

All of this took only seconds. Alva was fast with a gun. I, of course, had not ducked down as I had been instructed. I saw the windshield explode on the driver's side. Glass must have filled the cab of the truck. The driver must have ducked at the last second. He wasn't too drunk to duck. Immediately after the windshield exploded, I heard the distinctive sound of the Ford starter attempting to crank the engine to life. It roared to life with an open muffler and the throttle wide open. With the engine racing high and the driver bent over to avoid being shot, the truck was difficult to get into gear. After some gear grinding, which I could hear easily from our spot, the truck lurched into reverse and began an awkward retreat down the road backwards with the rear tires going, chirp, chirp, chirp as the rear wheels and driveline wound up and released trying to match the speed of the engine.

Alva stood up, carefully aimed without the benefit of the door rest, and put a round through the radiator of the truck. I saw the water begin squirting out the grille. The dual rear tires were catching up to the engine speed and all I could hear now was the sound of the exhaust as he went wide open in reverse and disappeared beyond the trees that lined the road. I could smell the smoke from the burned gunpowder. My Mother was screaming.

"Are you crazy? The police will be here any minute. Let's get out of here. Put that gun away".

Alva stood there a long minute. He was considering pursuing him. I knew what he was thinking. "Should I catch him and finish the job?" We heard more gear grinding. The truck must be turning around. Then we heard the exhaust, muffled by the trees, as he shifted through the gears and took off in the opposite direction.

Alva wanted to turn around and chase him down. My Mother was finally successful with her argument. She took full advantage of the situation. She knew she had the upper hand. She let go with all her protests. It finally worked. Alva put the Winchester back in the car on my back seat.

To me, he said, "Don't sit on that barrel. It might be hot. And next time I tell you to be still, don't keep moving around. You f**ked up my aim. I'd have got him before he ducked if the car wasn't shaking."

I had positioned myself so I could see out the back window. He was ready for the first shot before I was settled down.

There were no police. There were no charges filed on this incident. It just went away.

CHAPTER FORTY ONE

Finale

To hell with the consequences. I'm going to save my Mom

As for the general state of affairs at home, often, all seemed well during the day. There was work to keep everyone busy. I suppose that steady work kept worrisome things off Alva's mind. However, when night came it was frequently a different story. Something would trigger Alva into a rage during the night. I don't know if Alva was individually responsible for these tantrums or if my Mother instigated some of them. Either is possible. These episodes were frequent. The incidents became closer and closer together. One night, I'd chosen to sleep in the living room. I think I'd fallen asleep reading while lying on the sofa. Anyway, about midnight or later, I heard my Mom screaming. It seemed to me worse than other times. She seemed to be choking. She was screaming my name. It was like a dream only I wasn't waking up. It was real.

Mom was screaming, "Grant, get the gun. Make him stop. Make him stop."

Her words were barely intelligible. She was being choked. There was little doubt. The volume was lower on each word. Suddenly, the program kicked in that is built into all of us. It's the algorithm that kicks in when your Mother is being killed. At least that's how I have justified it to myself in later years. I jumped up, fully awake now. It's not a dream. I grabbed my little 22 rifle that always stood in the corner of the room. I rushed to the bedroom door, flipped on the light, found Alva and Mom, fully clothed, between the bed and the wall where they had fallen with him on top of her, hands around her throat and her screaming faintly. I was on autopilot but I knew I was going to protect my Mother.

I flipped the safety on the 22, lifted it to point directly at Alva and said, "Get off my Mom."

I only said it once. I only had to say it once. He turned and the look on his face spelled out his understanding of the situation. Alva was not a man to fear anything. But that's the closest I've ever seen him to fear.

He turned and said, "Put that gun down."

His eyes said, "Don't shoot."

He was out of breath from fighting my Mom. My Mom was out of breathe from being choked. She couldn't speak above a whisper. Alva started getting up.

He said, "Put that gun down before you shoot somebody. Put the safety back on."

Apparently he'd heard the safety click to fire.

My mind was made up. I was thinking in full auto mode now. Nothing or nobody could have stopped me at that point.

I said, "Get away from Mom."

He's yelling at me but he's getting up and backing away slightly. I am following his movement with the gun barrel. Mom is getting up. I'm not moving a muscle. The gun is against my shoulder and still pointed at Alva. Mom can't speak and can barely breathe. I can barely breathe. I think I arrived just in the nick of time. It took a long time before she could speak. Alva is yelling endless profanities at me now and telling me over and over to put the damn safety on. I haven't moved. I know I'm in deep trouble and I'm not moving until my Mom is out of harms way. I know I'm committed to the situation now. I'm going to see it through. Getting my Mom out of the room safely is job one. I felt like the only divider between my Mom's life and death was me and my gun. To hell with the consequences. I'm going to save my Mom. Finally, seemed like forever, she was able to get to her feet and walk beside me out the door of the bedroom. She went to the bedroom where I normally slept. Alva is still cussing me and telling me to put the gun down. Finally, I clicked the safety to off and moved backwards without lowering the gun. Alva stopped talking. I watched him but said nothing as I backed out of the bedroom. I backed away slowly until I reached the middle of the living room. I sat on the sofa where I'd been sleeping. I kept the gun across my legs. I was too scared to cry. But I sure wanted to cry. I sat there for a very long time. I wanted to relieve the emotion, all the various emotions that filled me like hot air in a thin balloon. I felt it coursing through me, but I had no provision for letting it out.

I could hear my Mom in the back bedroom coughing lightly once in a while and crying in between.

I sat watching the doorway. I wanted to reassure myself that Alva did not go down the short hallway to the back bedroom to 'finish the job'. He didn't.

Alva, occasionally, would say, "Grant, you put that damn gun down and put it away. Do you hear me?"

He didn't come out to see if I had followed his orders. I didn't answer him. I said not a word. I sat there all night on the sofa with my gun on my lap. I think I may have dozed off once or twice for a couple minutes. Sometimes I'd hear my Mom's cough after she quit crying.

I never cried. I couldn't cry a tear. Now, sixty years later, here I am writing about it and I can't keep from crying. Life is strange isn't it?

Next morning, I didn't need to wake up. I was already awake. I watched as it started getting daylight. I put the 22 away. I made my books ready for school. I ate some breakfast, alone. I woke my Mom up. She got up, got dressed and told me she wanted to leave. She wanted to go to her Father and Mother's home. She had had it with this existence.

Alva was still asleep. Mom was afraid to stay there with me gone to school. She told me so. She asked if I'd go next door and call her sister to come over and get her. We had no telephone. The Yancy's had a phone. I went next door before going to school. I made the call for her. I told them to come quickly because I had to catch the bus to school. They came and picked her up before I went to school. I can't remember the rest of that day. It's like a blur. I don't know if I went to school. Although, I never missed school, I can't remember going. Surely I must have for I remember coming home and no one was home.

Alva came home later as I was doing my homework. I always did my homework before doing other things. Alva didn't speak to me as he came into the house.

Later, as it was getting dark, he said, "Where's Gerene?"

I said, "She went to her dad's house."

He said, "How'd she get there."

I said, "I called them to come get her."

He said, "Where was I?"

I said, "Asleep."

He said, "It looks like she would have woke me up before she left. Did she say when she was coming back."

I said, "Yes.

Long pause.....

"Well, when did she say she was coming back?"

"She said, never."

Alva didn't answer. He just put on one of those far away looks.

Alva was aware of what he'd created the night before. Of course, there is no justification for choking someone like that. He never apologized to me. He never mentioned how close he came to getting shot. He never mentioned what had caused the argument between him and Mom. He never, ever discussed it again.

I wish he had. I wish he had revealed what drove him into such a fury. He never brought up the subject again.

My Mom came back briefly with her dad's truck to pick up her belongings. I believe the truck was a 1950 Chevrolet. She asked if I wanted to go with her. I refused. I didn't know what to do. I was torn. I was about 12. I chose to stay at our house. I think, now, that I was making a decision to stay with the house instead of staying with either of the parents. Like the feline attachment for the home, I was hanging onto the geography instead of the parents.

Alva wasted no time finding a girlfriend. I think she lived in Hot Springs. Whoever she may have been, she never came home with him. He spent most of his time in Hot Springs. I spent most of my time alone at home when I wasn't at school. I spent many evenings and nights with my old friends, my books.

Alva would be home sometimes for a week at a time. During those episodes, he expected me to help him with his whisky sales. I did. If he made a purchase, I'd accompany him. During the night, when he made a sale that required a trip into the woods and the old cemetery, I'd go along as backup and carry the gun. It was just a safety thing in case someone tried to rob him. When Alva would deliver some whisky, I would drive the car. I liked that. It was exciting for me. I cared little about the whisky. I certainly didn't drink it. I just wanted to drive the car. I loved sliding around those turns. Usually we planned the delivery so well that there was no need to race anyone to accomplish the delivery. In only a few instances were we chased and it was fun to be challenged. I was too young to be driving as I did. But, I didn't know that.

CHAPTER FORTY TWO

Whisky Lesson for Maggie

"Mr. Burris, I done sold all that whisky and all that baloney too."
Maggie

Alva had wasted no time getting back up to full speed in the whisky business after returning from jail. It was easier to resume that than resume the planting and animal husbandry he had practiced before. Now, with Mom gone, he had a missing team member. It suddenly changed things in multiple ways. He began actively soliciting the customers he knew. We made many deliveries when it was impractical for the customer to pick up the whisky. We charged more for delivered product. More was sold by delivery than picked up at the house. That eliminated the need for Alva to stay at home. And, consequentially, he was seldom home. About the only thing for which he came home was to sell some and make some deliveries. There were a few exceptions. I'll get to those.

One of those customers he developed was the black Namibian lady, named Maggie, who I described at the beginning of this story . She had a large family and, seemingly, could not get on her feet financially. Alva had sympathy for her and the enormous amount of kids.

He once told me, "She lets those black men come to her house and eat up all the food. Then the kids have nothing to eat. They are all just skin and bones. If I have a chance, I'm going to help her as much as I can. She doesn't know how to manage her money. With so many kids, there's, obviously, something else she fails to manage too."

His plan was to sell her some whisky on credit. That was very unusual for him because he never sold anything on credit. Usually, it was pay in advance.

On one of those visits to the Maggie's house, while I waited in the car, he explained in great detail to her how she should manage. He repeated his lesson to her, as he had taught it, after we were on our way.

Alva said, "I told her to buy a gallon. I'd finance her for it from Saturday morning until Monday morning. I said, buy a gallon and I will show you how to cut it (dilute it) with water to make the equivalent of two gallons. When it's diluted you can sell it in shot glasses for $1 each. I told her I'd give her money to buy a few shot glasses. I told her to buy a loaf of white bread, some mayonnaise and a package of baloney sausage. I showed her how to make a baloney sandwich. I showed her how she could sell the sandwiches for $1 each also. I said if she bought the whisky, I'd go get the bread and baloney and the shot glasses for her. She was surprised and interested. She had never thought of this. I told her that she was letting those lazy men eat all her food and starving her kids. I told her it made me feel bad to see them all starving while the men had plenty. I told her to run the men off unless they wanted to buy a shot or buy a sandwich. She seemed really interested. I picked up a kid's ball bat and handed it to her. I said, use this on them if they fail to behave."

Alva was happy to tell me all this. I was a bit surprised that he took such an interest in this lady. Something must have touched his heart. It must have been Maggie's condition with all those kids.

Alva repeated his trip to her house with me in the hot car watching all those kids. It took several trips before she had the routine down pat. Apparently, those numerous trips were coaching episodes. On the day she agreed, Alva was so happy that she was going to do it.

Alva said, "I can hardly believe it. She going to get a gallon tonight. She will cut it like I told her and sell the shots and sandwiches to those no account men that have been stealing from her. She said she'd use a baseball bat to keep them from stealing."

Alva was beside himself with joy. You would have thought he was a venture capitalist with a successful startup under his wing.

Alva said, "She was a little nervous but I told her I'd come by on Sunday morning early to see how she'd done. That seemed to make her feel better. I think she's smart but just never had anyone take an interest in her. Those men all take advantage of her but never provide for her. All they do is get her pregnant and eat her food. I hope I can change that. If she ever catches on to the technique, she will do well for herself and her kids."

That night, right on schedule, the walking delivery man showed up at our door. Alva had chosen someone he trusted and had financed the cost of the delivery which I believe was $2. Delivery man showed up. Alva delivered the gallon of whisky. We waited for Sunday morning to see how she did with it. Delivery was done on Friday night in preparation for the Saturday night sale. Alva drove by on Saturday morning to make sure it arrived as expected. It had. He took the loaf of bread, baloney, mayonnaise and shot glasses as he made the Saturday morning check up call on Maggie. All was ready for Saturday night.

Sunday morning I rode with Alva as we checked out the new business venture. It as about 9 AM when we arrived. Maggie was waiting at the door of the old ram-shackled shotgun house. No kids were in sight. They were still asleep. She was all smiles. Of course, she always seemed to be all smiles with that overbite of hers. This morning was special. We could see before the car stopped rolling that she had a roll of money in her hand. Maggie was all teeth and laughing and came out to the car.

She said, "Mr. Burris, I done sold all that whisky and all that baloney too. I did just what you said and didn't have no trouble at all. It was easy. Easy. I picked up my ball bat and I just said, see that bat. Want some of that.... or want some of this. And I showed 'em a sandwich that I had already made."

She said, "He grinned and said, I believe I will have the sandwich."

She said, "I said, then give me a dollar before you start to eatin'. He did and it was fine after that. He told one of his friends and they both came back for a couple shots and another sandwich for his friend."

She was so happy. She said, "It just kept on all night like that. Just like you said."

Maggie had a fist full of dollar bills. She said, "I needs you to count it for me. I never learned to count Mr. Burris."

Alva was laughing. He wasn't laughing at her. He was laughing for her. She had been holding the money clenched in her hand so long, that it was sweaty and stuck together. She probably had it in her hand all night. Alva took it from her hand and counted the money back into her hand from his one bill at a time, slowly. He made her repeat the numbers as he said them.

Alva counted the dollars one by one. Maggie repeated the numbers. Some, she pronounced poorly. It was all one dollar bills because she said she refused to make change. She didn't know how. Alva counted $74. The woman said she had never had that much money in her entire life. I believe it. She acted like she had won the lottery. She was laughing and squealing and spinning around. I loved it. It was a happy moment, for sure.

Alva got out of the car and went in with her. I stayed in the car as usual. Alva said later he found a good place for her to hide the money. He took his $10 for the gallon of whisky. He may have taken the money for the bread and baloney. I have forgotten. It was very little. After he was satisfied that she had hid the money where no one could find it, we left.

On a return visit, a week or so later, we stopped at our place in front of the shotgun house. The kids were all playing outside in the usual fashion. Maggie called one of the little girls as Alva got out of the car.

Maggie pulled on the arm of one of the little girls and pointed at Alva. She said, "You go give Mr. Burris a hug. He the one that showed me how to make the money that bought that dress you got on."

The little girl ran to Alva and looking like a little black spider with her spindly arms and legs, threw them around Alva's leg. Alva continued walking as she hung on. He walked toward Maggie slowly with the one stiff leg that the little girl was riding on. Alva looked by at me and grinned real big. Then he continued walking on toward Maggie with his stiff legged walk. That little girl hung on for the ride with all her arms and legs wrapped around Alva's left leg. Alva was happy. I didn't need an explanation for the happiness. I understood it easily. That little girl had gone from nude to clothed with one lesson from Alva. I felt proud that he had helped them. All the kids seemed to want to cluster a little closer to him that morning than ever before. Their invented game was strangely unimportant. The little girl kept hanging on his leg for the longest time. I fully understood what he had done for this family. Alva had 'taught them to fish'. I believe they understood his gesture of help on a deeper level than I could. So many years later that I'm remembering it and it puts a happy tear in my eye. I'm still very proud of that morning and Alva.

CHAPTER FORTY THREE

Lawrence House

The first trip to the lake taught me a lot.

Alva decided one summer that he was going to drive to Arizona. I'm sure it involved a girlfriend. His trips alone always involved a woman. He never explained it.

He simply said, "I'm going on a trip and I think you should stay with the Lawrences until I return. I was glad to get a chance to stay with them. Harold and his wife, Dauphine, were fun to be around. Dauphine had a younger sister named Pat. Pat lived with Harold and Dauphine and was dating a friend of mine, Donald Lackey. Donald had been my friend since the fourth grade. He remains one of my closest friends today.

This was a great opportunity for me to hang out with some friends without fearing Alva's anger regarding the whisky business. Dauphine and Pat's father had been involved in the whisky business for years. His name was Frank Smith. He had been captured and imprisoned many times. His only crime, to my knowledge, was distilling moonshine whisky. Because Alva was aware of that, he was more tolerant of me being with this group than others. The Lawrences neither made nor sold whisky. They only consumed it.

Harold had a ski boat and he loved using it. Unfortunately, he loved to drink too. He was never violent but he did become heavily intoxicated frequently. This made driving and the operation of the boat rather risky. When he became so intoxicated that others began telling him to let someone else drive, he would hand it over to me. He would ask me to drive the car or the boat. The motivation was not always his alcohol level. Often he simply wanted more time to make out with whom ever happened to be along. There were always numerous girls who wanted to go skiing in the summer. The boat was a magnet. Harold was a handsome guy. He was about 35 or 40. Easygoing. Quiet. Dark wavy hair. Muscular. The girls seemed unable to get enough of Harold and his toys. Most of the girls were 15 -17. I had no idea until a few 'parties' were complete, just how well Harold was scoring with those girls. The first trip to the lake taught me a lot. What a lesson.

The first stop, with the boat in tow, was to get gas. We always had a large cooler filled with beer and soft drinks when we left home. I would typically have one beer. I disliked being 'drunk'. They drank all the way to the destination. I wanted to be sharp and alert. If drugs had been available that made me sharper and more intently focused, I would likely have become addicted to them. At the first stop Harold switched places. He got in the back with a girl and I continued driving with the boat in tow. Harold never wasted time. Sometimes, by the time we reached the lake, he and the girls had drank more than they should have.

The likelihood of that was more than 'sometimes'. Usually, Harold had done more in the light of day than he should have with a girl half his age. The girls needed no instructions. No one in the car protested. No one stared. No one cared. Everyone acted as though this was old hat to them. I felt as though I was the only one surprised. I didn't reveal my surprise. I was driving. So, I acted as though everything was all ok. Normal stuff for me too. Of course. There was three modes of behavior. The one at home, the one in the car and the one in the boat. All were close to the same. It was.... anything goes.

By the time we reached the lake, Harold would barely be able to stand and the girl would often be asleep or passed out in the back seat. It's hard to tell the difference between those two conditions. Harold would throw a towel over her if she had shed her swimsuit during the trip. Usually, they had. He'd smile at me and stumble around to the boat, climb aboard it and ask me to back the boat down the ramp so that it could be launched. Harold had a nonchalant, easy going manner that defied all that had been happening on the way to the lake. He personified the 'helpful coach' who always knew just what to do next. Once he was aboard he took on a new life. He would seem stunningly sober again although he had trouble looking directly at you. I would back the new Ford station wagon down the ramp, get the boat into the water and Harold would take over. As he and the boat floated away from the trailer, he would busy himself with getting the outboard started so that he could motor back to the dock to pick up all the remaining girls and me. It was like he had drank nothing. He was at home in that boat. I would pull the wagon and trailer out of the water and, if lucky, find the shade of a tree to park the car under. I would check on the girl lying in the back seat to make sure she was covered. Sometimes, I would call her name. If there was no response, I would leave her there in the shade. If there was others in the car, we would all go to the dock, meet Harold with the boat and take off for some skiing. We were all kids. I was the youngest. Harold was the only adult. Harold, seemingly sober, would ask if anyone wanted to ski.

"Who wants to ski first?"

If no one offered to jump in, Harold would throw out the rope, jump in, swim to the rope and get the skis on. The boat was still running. Harold would say, "Grab the wheel, Grant." I'd get under the wheel and stretch out the rope for him. Harold was a good skier even when intoxicated. He'd get up on the first try, always. I'd do about 35. That was close to wide open with a load of girls and a skier. That was fun.

After a while we would stop to let him rest. He would get in the boat and head back to the dock. He wanted to check on the girl we had left in the back seat. When we arrived at the dock, Harold would tell us to wait while he went to check on our friend in the back seat of the wagon. Typically, the girl would be awake. Harold would return shortly with his arm around her or carrying her. He'd help her into the boat and off we'd go on another round. Harold was the consummate gentleman during these trips. He was always concerned about everyone's happiness. Even when he was obviously intoxicated, his first concern was the happiness of others. No, maybe that's not completely correct. His first concern was his own happiness. The second concern was that of others. I was repeatedly surprised with the absence of resistance he encountered while having his way with any girl who happened to be along and wanted to be in the back seat. While in the middle of the lake it was common for everyone to strip off their suits and swim naked for a while. A lot of stuff went on under the water blanket.

Today, much of the activity would be classified as molestation in some form. Perhaps it would be called molestation of a minor or statutory rape or contribution to the delinquency of a minor. The charges would likely go on and on. To us, it was just a day at the lake. No one went home as 'damaged goods'. I was about 13. The girls were all at least one year older than me. Some were four years older. Harold, of course, was the adult. Harold was the creative one. He was always inventing new ways to have fun with girls. It was nice to be in an environment where there were no restrictions on anything. There were no drugs. Only beer. And sex. Anything was OK except violence. Maybe we were the first hippies and didn't know it. Contrary to what many psychologist would say, I think no one was damaged by any of this. The behavior that professionals would condemn was actually a 'vacation experience' to me. It was a calming break from the rigid abusive routine to which I was so accustomed. There was hardly any profanity and everyone just had fun and there was never a negative day. That was a great summer for me.

I lived with Harold and Dauphine for most of the summer. They had a very nice modern house. I had my own bedroom. There was running water and electric lights. How much better could it get? I enjoyed my stay with them. I was treated with respect and included in all their outings. They made me feel as though I was a part of their family. They all knew I was from a moonshine family and it didn't matter to them. It was a very enjoyable summer and a big break from the whisky business that I had grown to despise. I grew up a lot during that summer in many ways. I truly thank Harold and Dauphine for having me at their house during that summer.

There were many trips that summer, to the preferred swimming holes on the creeks that only a few of us knew about. Some of the swimming holes were great. They were almost like someone had designed them with great rocks along the side to jump from. One had a swing, a rope that allowed you to swing out over the water and drop in. On those trips it was just us kids. Those trips were different than when Harold was along. However, it was mostly the same girls. The difference was there were teenage guys along. Most of the guys preferred to act macho instead of having sex. Some kissing was all they were capable of. They thought that was really cool. They didn't know what they were missing. The girls were way more mature than the guys. I was the youngest of the group, but I'd probably seen more than any of them. I also was better at keeping the secrets. That meant everyone's secrets.

CHAPTER FORTY FOUR

First Car

I had a million plans. They all centered around a car

By now, I was about 14. Alva was home one day and asked me if I had any plans for the day. I said I did not. He asked if I'd like to go driving around to see if we could find a car for me. I was so surprised.

He said, "I promised you I'd buy you a car when you turned 14 and I want to keep my promise to you."

I answered, "Sure, I'd like to do that. Thanks."

He said, "Let's go down to Arkadelphia and look around for one you might like."

I said, "Great. I'm ready right now."

Actually, I had been ready for about a year.

We drove to Arkadelphia which is about 20 miles south of Malvern. I'm unsure why he chose Arkadelphia. Little Rock was a much bigger town and that's where he usually went to shop for a car. Alva knew that I had my heart set on a 1950 black Chevy. I talked about it whenever someone would listen.

Alva must have seen the car we found prior to our trip. As we passed by a car lot on the outskirts of town he said, "Isn't that a car like you have been wanting?"

It was a black 1951 Chevrolet. I couldn't believe it. He had seen it first. Normally, I would spot all the cool cars and was unable to get him to look at them. No doubt he'd seen this car and was simply parading me by it as though it was a surprise. Well, it certainly was. We turned off the road and returned to the dealership that displayed the car.

Alva said, "Why don't you look it over and see if you think it's one like you wanted."

I said, "I know it is already. It's just what I've been wanting."

He said, "Well, let's go find a salesman and see if he will let us take it for a drive. You can drive it and see if you like it."

I could hardly breathe. I was about to have my own car. Alva found a salesman and they talked for a bit. He arranged for us to go for a drive. The excitement was nearly more than I could bear. I got behind the wheel and we pulled out onto the highway. Alva was giving instructions regarding the speed and telling me to watch for the traffic. I'd driven plenty but never in a car that could possibly be mine within a few minutes. A black '51 Chevy. I couldn't believe it.

We made a short drive and returned in about 10 minutes.

Alva said, "Do you think you'd like this one?"

I answered, "Yes."

Alva said, "Well, let's go back and see how much he will take for it."

Wow. That sounded really good to me. Any price would have been cheap.

Alva talked with the salesman for a bit and easily got him to agree to $200. I was so happy that I could hardly breathe. My own car. Now I could get a job and drive to work. I had a million plans. They all centered around a car.

It was very handy to have my own car. I appreciated Alva purchasing it for me. Most of the first few days afterwards, I simply looked at it and tried to imagine all the things I was going to do. I had a fertile imagination. I imagined trips that I would take and how much fun I would have traveling. I imagined I could go almost anywhere.

We had purchased it on Saturday. That gave me all weekend to clean and polish it so that I could drive it to school on Monday. It needed some cleaning. I could hardly sleep at night. I chose to sleep in our front room on the sofa so that I could look out at it any time I woke up during the night. I woke up plenty. I may not have slept. I was at that window checking it out all night long.

The next morning I told Alva how happy I was with it. He seemed genuinely pleased that I was proud of it.

He said, "I told you a long time ago that when you got your driver's license I'd buy you a car like you like. I wanted to keep my word to you and also to teach you that when you give someone your word you must keep that promise no matter how difficult it is for you to do it."

He observed me to make sure I was paying attention. I certainly was. He said, "This was as much a lesson to you as it was a gift to you. Be sure to remember that. It was a gift to you because you have always tried to help me when I asked and you have kept yourself out of trouble at school and otherwise. You have made good grades although I wasn't educated enough to help you with your studies. I want you to know that I'm very proud of that. This car is a way for me to say thank you. For as long as you remember this first car, let it remind you that I'm proud of you."

I said, "Thank you" again and I truly meant it. I am still appreciative today of that lesson and of that gift, my first car.

CHAPTER FORTY FIVE

Trip to California

I had been at the wheel over 24 hours

Alva surprised me by asking if I wanted to take a trip to California. This was during the period after I had gotten my car but before I'd taken a job. Sometimes when he was home, he and I would go visit his sister Dora. I enjoyed those times and Aunt Dora. Alva seemed to like and trust her and her son, Harold.

During one of those visits, Alva and Dora began talking about California. Alva, out of the blue, said he thought that he and I would take a trip to California in search of 'work'.

He said, "Grant and I have been talking about it and I think that during the summer while he is out of school we should go out there and see if I can find a job. I'm getting tired of this whisky business."

Dora agreed. Harold agreed. Both had lived in California for a brief period. I agreed because I saw it as an opportunity to drive a lot. Plus, I wanted to see California.

The deal was made. Harold would go into town and check on our house sometimes. We would write often to update them on where we were. We would take my car, the little 1951 Chevy. I would get to drive all I wanted to. This seemed great.

Alva and I set the date to leave. We left from Dora's house with all our stuff packed inside my Chevy. I also took along a small pet tortoise that I had cared for approximately a year. We left early in the morning just after daylight. This was Alva's plan.

We drove to Dallas, Texas on the first day. It was late in the afternoon when we passed through the Dallas/Ft. Worth area. Alva said we should drive all the way to El Paso, Texas as he had done before, if I felt up to it. I loved all this driving. I was up to it easily. About midnight, I wondered if I was going to be able to stay awake. I'd been driving about 18 hours. I was rapidly developing tunnel vision where everything looks alike. All I was seeing was the center line in the road. Alva wouldn't let me drive over 55 mph. That was about as fast as that Chevy would go without risk of failure anyway. We drove all night, then the sun came up at our backs. How big was Texas anyway? Bigger than I had imagined, for sure. I was still driving at 9 AM and very tired. I had been at the wheel over 24 hours. I was having trouble staying awake. Alva, as a tribute to him, had not slept either. We were both tired. Alva kept talking to me to keep me awake. It was good that he did. I was very sleepy but determined to make it to El Paso. I was struggling heavily with fatigue. West Texas highways are very boring.

About 1 PM we entered the city limits of El Paso. I had been watching the signs as they told in decreasing increments how far we were from the city. It seemed that those last miles went by so slowly. We entered El Paso and immediately began looking for a motel to spend the night (evening and night). It was early afternoon. We selected one and Alva went inside to pay and get the room key. It was a nice room with two beds. Most of all it had a nice bathtub. I could hardly wait to get into that bathtub and soak. I was so tired. Alva invited me to take a bath first. I did. If felt wonderful. I think I soaked for about thirty minutes. Alva was next. When he was clean, he came out. We went to the local restaurant, ate our dinner and returned to our room. We went to bed immediately. How wonderful that bed felt. I will never forget it. The time was about 6 PM I believe. It was still daylight outside. I just wanted to shut my eyes, finally.

During the night, Alva woke me after shaking me a long time. He said it was getting daylight and that we needed to get up and get on the road.

Alva said, "The sun is coming through the window and it woke me up. So, we'd better get up and get going. They will be kicking us out of here pretty soon if we don't get moving."

I got up, dressed and we made preparations to continue driving. When we went outside, I said, "The sun isn't up. It's night."

Alva said, "Well, I don't know what happened. The sunshine was shining through the window so bright that it woke me up. I pulled back the shades and looked out. It was so bright that I couldn't look at it. It certainly wasn't a car light because it was up above the buildings. I thought we had overslept and that it was about 8 o'clock."

Alva was confused by all this. I checked my watch. It showed about 2 AM. Alva was convinced that my watch must have stopped or something. He insisted that we get going. We did. We took off down the road. I was hungry and asked if we could stop at a Denny's restaurant that we were approaching. Alva agreed. I pulled in. We had a nice 'breakfast'.

I drove for a couple hours. Soon, I was feeling tired like I had not slept enough. It was not getting daylight as Alva had expected it to. We drove for a long time. Finally, I asked Alva if we could stop, anywhere, and let me sleep in the car until it was daylight. I was beat. Alva was still baffled by how we had gotten confused. He had gotten confused on the 'sun coming up' while at the motel.

I didn't care about much at that point. I just wanted to sleep for a while. I found a nice gas station, in the middle of nowhere in the desert. I pulled alongside it, parked and closed my eyes immediately. We were well into New Mexico at this point. I slept until I woke. The sun was up. That woke me. There was no doubt this time. It was definitely the sun. It was summer and we were in New Mexico. It was hot.

I woke Alva and we went took turns going into the gas station bathroom to take care of business and to wash our eyes. Soon, we were on the road again after filling our tank.

Just to recap here: We had left Arkansas on Thursday morning. We drove all day, all night and on Friday afternoon got a motel in El Paso. Alva woke up prematurely, woke me up and we began driving again on the same night we went to bed. We drove for the remainder of that Friday night/Saturday morning, went to sleep by the gas station early on Saturday morning. All that is pretty certain. We woke up just after sunup on Saturday morning, washed up, ate breakfast and continued down the road.

Now comes the strange part. As we drove west along the road, (not all was Interstate freeway back then), we began to notice that people were attending church services at every church we passed. All had big crowds in front. At first we thought maybe it was a wedding in progress. Then we began to wonder if the churches we were seeing was a denomination that worshipped on Saturday instead of Sunday. We each mentioned this to each other. We agreed that it was unusual to find so many worshipping on Saturday. We agreed to observe the name of the next church. We did. It was a conventional Catholic Church. It was being attended as though it was Sunday. We were very confused by this. Church after church it was the same story.

Soon noon arrived and we were getting hungry. We stopped at a restaurant. It was likely another Denny's. There were so many of them along the road and Alva really liked them. "They keep your coffee cup full".

While we were eating, Alva called the server over during our meal.

He said, "Pardon me. It sounds like a foolish question. We have been traveling and we are unsure of some things. We saw a lot of people going to church as we drove along and were confused why they would doing that on Saturday."

The server, known as a 'waitress' during that era, said, "Sir, this is Sunday, not Saturday."

Alva said, "Is it really?"

She said, "All day". And gave us a big smile.

Alva and I could not believe what we had just heard. We stared at each other without speaking. I don't know which of us was more perplexed with that statement. We began to map out where we had been on each day. We traced our path from Arkansas to where we were including our time in the motel and Alva's mistake regarding when we woke up. We traced everything over and over, painstakingly, and could not make sense of our 'Missing Day'. We discussed it many times over the years and could never determine how we lost a day.

Alva was meticulous about keeping up with the time, the elapsed time, the day of the week, and even the lunar cycles. He was always cognizant of these things. He always kept a small calendar with him to mark off the days. I was not so much so. I kept up with the time of the day, of course but on this item, I was in complete agreement with him. We lost a day and never could attribute it to anything.

Our trip continued into and through California. We went as far north as Fresno and as far south as San Diego. We traveled north and south along Highway 1. Going through Orange County and specifically, Laguna Beach, was a treat. I promised myself that someday I would come back to live in this locality near the ocean. With help from others, I kept my promise.

Our job search was unproductive. I was too young and too inexperienced to acquire a job of substantial nature. Alva was unskilled in most areas. He tried very hard but determined that he would have to join a union to acquire a job.

After much traveling, which was enjoyable to me, we agreed to return to Arkansas and mark this off as a nice vacation. I enjoyed my time with Alva. It was the first and longest time we had spent together. I felt we kind of got to know each other during this trip. He maintained the dominant alpha male position as he had always done. I accepted that. We talked a lot. I came no closer to understanding his violent flares of temper than I had understood before the trip. However, during this trip, there were no instances of violence.

We never solved the missing day issue although we talked about it frequently. I have thought about it repeatedly since it happened. I am still unsure of what happened. One thing is for sure, it was not a random mistake by two sleepy guys. We simply, individually, could not account for what happened to Saturday.

CHAPTER FORTY SIX

Return to Malvern

"Don't let anybody shoot me. And most of all, don't you shoot me." Alva Burris

Our trip was over and there would not be another one together for many years. Not until I was married and living in California many years later did he and I take a long trip together. During that one, the roles had been reversed and it was a great trip to Canada in a new 1971 Buick GS that I still own.

When we returned from the California trip Alva began his whisky business again. He determined that it was the only way he could make any money. We still had the house on Babcock Street. Since I'd had more experience with driving and had more or less proven myself during the California trip, he allowed me to do a lot more driving during the whisky deliveries. I hated the whisky business but I loved the fast driving.

Since my vision was better than his at night, I always did the night driving. The deliveries of whisky to our location was normally performed by the seller. The seller would hire a person to deliver to us. He'd deliver to a designated spot on the property. The spot was called the 'gravel pit'. The area had been bulldozed out years before to build the road, I believe. Alva had the area well groomed for the deliveries. A tree top was pulled across the dim road that led to the fence where the delivery vehicle was to pull into our property. The driver knew the property. The driver's signal from us was, if the tree is moved from the dim road, then it's OK to deliver the load. If the tree is in the road, don't deliver for whatever reason. Alva would only move the tree after he had scouted around prior to the delivery to make sure that no one was watching us. Every delivery went perfect, always. Each delivery was done on schedule.

My job during the delivery was to stand at a distance without being detected. I was to carry the 38 automatic pistol and hold the 12 gauge shotgun. Alva's instructions were clear. "Don't let anybody shoot me. And most of all, don't you shoot me."

I was confident of my ability to guard him. I had spent considerable time already guarding my Mother when she would deliver whisky by the gallon to customers while Alva was in jail. I was completely comfortable with my role as a guard for Alva. I had proven my marksmanship to Alva on numerous occasions. He was comfortable with my ability to handle a firearm.

Alva and the driver of the delivery car would unload the five gallon jugs of whisky. It didn't take too long for the two of them to unload the car. The back seat was filled with jugs as well as the trunk compartment. Some of the vehicles used for delivery had the structure between the back seat and the trunk removed so that jugs could be stacked all the way from front to back on a big load. The drivers were always a bit on the crazy side. Alva was adamant to them that they never spin the tires or behave in an erratic manner when near the unloading area.

Alva would tell them each time, "Don't act crazy when you are around here. Don't attract attention to yourself. Act like nothing is happening until you are well away from here. Then you can do whatever you want. Just never attract attention to this area."

Those instructions were followed almost to the letter. On one delivery, after the load was unloaded, I walked out, as usual, to be a little closer to Alva while he carried the five's to their hiding places. I wasn't on the delivery scene but I could watch it easily. Alva was by the cluster of five's getting ready to pick up one when the driver of the delivery car reached the main gravel road. As he exited the gravel pit area he gunned the engine and spun the tires getting onto the road. It was not necessary. He was digging two big ruts that began in the gravel pit and reached out onto the road. I was surprised. I had just heard Alva tell him to drive easy until he was well away from the area.

Alva jerked around at the sound of the tires digging into that gravel and the sound of the engine revving. The driver had just straightened out on the main gravel road. The car was still spinning the tires. Alva let out with a group of expletives that described the driver's heritage and how God should treat him if they should meet.

Alva said to me, "Grant, put a load in that car."

I knew what he meant. I didn't hesitate. I put a load of 00 buckshot in the side of the passenger's door. The driver let off the gas immediately and then it seemed he got on it harder than before. He really spun the tires and took off.

Alva said, "If I see that son of a bitch again, I'll break his damn neck. I'm going to tell (seller's name omitted) that to never send that crazy bastard down here again."

"It's crazy people like that who get someone caught. He's got no sense. That makes me mad. You sure got a load in the side of that car quick. That was good. It was a long shot but I believe you put the whole load in the door. I'm going to tell (seller) that it's the guy driving the car with the buckshot in the side. That should teach him something. He was just mad because I cautioned him to be careful and not to arouse attention. He was showing off. Now, he can showoff that car with the holes in it to his boss. He'll probably lose his job over this."

Alva continued to compliment me on being there to support him. He would also say, "I don't want you to ever have anything to do with the whisky business. It's a dangerous way to make a living. I want something better for you."

However, here I was guarding for his whisky business, shooting people on cue and helping to deliver to all parts of town. Yet, he 'didn't want me to get involved in the whisky business'. This is part of that paradox that I keep coming back to. It is part of what I had to adjust to as I tried to find my way through, what I later considered, the maze. That night, in the woods, I was happy to have pleased Alva, happy to have received his compliments and gave no thought much else.

CHAPTER FORTY SEVEN

Alva's Girlfriend

It changed my opinion of him.

Alva began regular and prolonged visits with his new girlfriend. Although my Mother, earlier, had told me he had a girlfriend, I refused to believe it. Now, with him gone so much, his absence demanded that I face the truth. I suppose I had known all along. I can't remember when I fully made up my mind.

I think it may have been when my niece, Delores, said, "Grant, he couldn't be gone so much if he wasn't sleeping somewhere. He must have a girlfriend."

From the day she said that, I began to face the facts. The truth finally found its way into my naive thinking. I began to plan what I must do to learn the truth. I thought about it until one of those times he was leaving to be gone no telling how long. I guess I'd already decided. I was going to follow him. When he left the house, I waited for a bit, got into my car and caught up behind him on the road. I had gas in my car and I was determined to see where he went. I was nervous. I had an idea what he would do if he caught me. I didn't want to be caught.

He left our house on Babcock Street and headed toward Hot Springs. Seems like all his roads always took him to Hot Springs. I followed at a safe distance but did not let him out of my sight. Soon we were in Hot Springs and in a part of town where I had waited in the car for long periods of time when I was younger. He was parked near a house where my Mother and I had waited on him many times. I parked near the place so that I could cover him getting out of the car. I shut off my lights and watched. Soon he and a woman, a much younger woman, came out, got into the car together and took off. The woman was sitting against him as they left. There was no doubt, this was the girlfriend that my Mother had worried about. It was the girlfriend he had had all the while he accused my Mother of unfaithfulness. I was very nervous. This was a revelation. I followed them to a restaurant where they were intending to eat. I was never seen. I waited while they ate or did whatever they came for. When they left, I followed them back to her house. I waited for a while a distance away. I had driven the last little bit with no lights so that I would not be detected. After a while, I eased by the house but could not see inside. I parked again and waited. I waited until the lights went out. Then I headed for home. I knew, finally, that he had had a girlfriend the entire time. Finally, I knew.

I returned home. Alva was gone for days. It was perhaps 2 weeks before he came home. I said nothing to him about my adventure and discovery. I never mentioned it, ever. It changed my opinion of him. I knew, finally, that my Mother had been right and that he was doing the thing he had been accusing her of doing. It made a little sense for him to be paranoid about my Mother's faithfulness. He knew that if he had the opportunity he would be behaving as he had accused my Mother of behaving. I thought this was worse than anything he could have accused her of doing. However, I had few choices. I could not confront him with the facts because he would likely do what he had threaten, kick me out on the street. I needed a home to live in while I finished school. I decided to try to reestablish contact with my Mother who now was remarried and lived in Shreveport, Louisiana. I determined that as soon as school was over I was going to go live with her if she would allow it. On the night I returned from Hot Springs I made up my mind that I was destined to leave Alva and all his whisky business, forever. I was able to follow my plan, eventually, when I finished school.

CHAPTER FORTY EIGHT

The Chase

Whisky was in the back. We were loaded and under way.

Not many kids had the opportunity to experience the emotions that I did under the conditions that I have described. Many of those experiences tempered my future reactions to problems. After seeing life at the seediest level possible, some of the experiences likely diluted my ability to trust others. One thing that certainly happened, it increased my driving ability.

Alva always trusted my night vision. His vision had been reduced by age and by an injury to his left eye when he was a small boy. That combination left him with less than stellar vision. Perhaps that's the reason he appreciated my willingness to drive at night when there was whisky to deliver. Whatever the reason, when he asked if I wanted to drive a load to a customer, I was quick to accept. First it meant that I was pleasing him, which was often difficult. Second, it meant I would get to drive. I loved driving. Unknown to him, when I was alone on the back roads, I practiced my slides and turns. I had practiced the run up to my Aunt Dora's house which was about 10 miles of dirt road with plenty of curves. I charted a map of the road to her house and had each turn rated for maximum speed. I crudely mapped entry and exit speeds from each turn. It was great fun. It was good experience and relatively safe because of the absence of traffic.

The experience was always there if needed during a whisky delivery. Most of our whisky runs were calm but we always had to be on guard for a sheriff's car that might try to corner us. This was one of those nights.

Alva sold five gallons of whiskey in one gallon jugs. That meant three sacks. Two gallons in each of two sacks and one gallon in a sack alone. Alva would carry two gallons in his left hand and three in his right hand. That meant he only made one trip to the car and then upon arrival at the destination, he made only one trip to the door of the house while I kept the engine running in the car. The entire delivery when done correctly only took a few seconds at the destination.

On this night, we had a delivery to make that required some driving on a dirt back road and some on a paved road. Our routine often consisted of using dirt back roads to avoid the heavily traveled major highways. This reduced the amount of time on a public road and lowered the risk of an encounter with the police. In addition to this, we never made a delivery twice using the same path. We altered the route to the destination each time even when it entailed a much longer drive.

This delivery was intended for a customer near Donaldson, a small town south of Malvern. Donaldson was a straight shot down Highway 67, the route that reached all the way to Texarkana and beyond. However, to avoid the main road, we traveled the back roads. We had previously made a dry run in the daytime so that we would know exactly where we were going. This was customary so that we could familiarize ourselves with the route. We also mapped out alternate ways to get home if we were trapped with a roadblock. The plans were made well but the location and activities of the police were always the unknown.

On this night we were driving our 1955 Oldsmobile. Great car. Five gallons packaged as I described would fit perfectly on the back floor board. Since it was a four door, the entrance and exit with the whisky was easy for Alva. We drove to the gravel pit near our house, I kept the engine running with no lights while Alva loaded the previously sacked jugs. I used the parking brake for stopping so no brake lights signaled our stop. It only took a minute or so for him to dash out into the woods from the parking spot, get the five gallons and set them in the back floor board ahead of the rear seat. The floor was flat and they were secure there. Alva got back into the car, careful not to slam the door. He would reclose the door after we were under way. The whole idea was to make no noise, if possible. I drove easily back onto the dirt road that ran by the gravel pit. I thought about the delivery guy whose car I had put a round of buckshot into as he entered the road at the same place. I needed no encouragement to drive softly. Whisky was in the back. We were loaded and under way.

I drove up the road at a reasonable speed that would attract no attention. I turned right onto a secondary road, making my way to the old Sand Road that would take me around Malvern. All was well. We met no cars. There were no cars behind us. All important attributes for a successful run. I hit the Sand Road and followed it around town so that I could get onto the Ridge Road headed south. I had to make a short trip on 67, the paved road, until I could get off again. Pulling onto the paved road was always a tense time. Any police car noticing a car entering 67 from a secondary dirt road would attract attention. No cars were visible. I entered with no lights. We transitioned easily and traveled at the speed limit until we reached the dirt road we needed to transition to the Ridge Road. We made our transition, traveled easily along the dirt road until we reached the Ridge Road. The Ridge Road was paved but it was a secondary road. Alva felt it was a safer route than traveling straight through town. We made all our turns correctly and met no traffic that would arouse Alva's suspicion.

Down the Ridge Road and then a 90 degree turn off onto a dirt road that likely had a name, but I can't remember it. I just knew where it was and where it went. Many of the small dirt roads had a name that came from some family name who had lived on it years before. This one's name I did not know, but I was familiar with it.

We turned onto it and now we were on our final leg of the delivery. No more paved roads until we delivered. Alva breathed a sign of relief as we made our 90 degree turn on to this last road.

Alva said, "Well, if we don't see any cars, we will be finished pretty soon. Keep a close watch for any cars parked just off the road. That could mean a trap. We haven't delivered here before, so be very careful. Watch the little side roads for anyone backed up into one of them. If they are backed in, that means they plan to get away quick. It could be somebody who wants to catch us."

We traveled easily along the dirt road without any encounter. There was no dust from a previous car. All was calm. We were nearly finished.

When we were within a half mile of the destination, I shut off the lights and drove slowly for a bit. There were tall trees on either side the road we were on. Alva and I, earlier when it was light, had noticed a couple of little log roads, unmaintained, that were between our current location and our destination. We were watching each of those as I rolled along without lights.

Alva, with his seeming sixth sense for danger, said, "Let's just pause for a moment and look before we pull up to the house. We were already about 20 minutes later than we had told the customer to expect us. That was deliberate on Alva's part. He thought the added time would throw off any plan of a trap that might be in the works. One of Alva's tactics that had served him well was to pause and size up a situation rather than to burst in. His pause at the whisky still years earlier had likely saved his life and certainly avoided his capture. He had gleaned some of his skills from hunting. He often cautioned me when hunting to be quite and very patient.

He had said, "Walk quietly. Every now and then stop and listen for a bit. You'll be a lot more lucky if you do."

So we sat, alongside the road, lights off, engine running, waiting. Neither of us made a sound. We didn't talk. Our windows were down. Each of us tuned to the same sounds. The night was quite except for the soft idle of our Oldsmobile. Our nerves were tense but we knew exactly what we were waiting for. We were waiting for Alva to relax and give the go ahead. Soon, he would say, "Let's go ahead."

I was expecting Alva's signal to continue, but it didn't come. We waited longer than I had expected. Just as I was about to question the extra time, I heard an engine start.

Alva said, "Was that a car starting?"

I answered, "Yes. Up the road a ways."

Alva said, "Wait. See who it is."

I saw a car entering the road from the left with no lights. It turned right and was headed straight at us. It had a noticeable bulge on the roof. It was Police. It was a Sheriff's car.

I said one word, "Police."

Alva said, "You sure?"

"Yes."

Alva said, "Turn your lights on and ease on by. It's likely a trap. If it is, they will have the road blocked ahead of us. So, the only way out will be back the way we came."

My heart was beating fast and I was thinking of what I'd need to do. Just as our Oldsmobile was shifting into another gear, so were my reflexes. I eased ahead as I reached down and turned on my lights. The lights from the opposing car came on at almost the same time as mine. It likely surprised him. I saw his brake lights flare behind him as I turned my lights on. He had touched the brake momentarily in surprise but he didn't stop.

We met like two ships in the dark. I had already hit the gas and was accelerating forward when we met. Due to the terrain, a small knoll was behind me. The police car dropped over that knoll shortly after we met. His lights disappeared as he passed the peak of the knoll. I was doing 30 mph or so by this time.

Alva yelled, "Turn around quick. The road will be blocked on the other side of the house just like it was on this side. They will expect us to be trapped in the middle."

I pulled slightly to the right to give me a little room, pressed the emergency brake lightly with my left foot, applied it at same time I turned the wheel to the left. The 55 Olds was one of the first years to have the emergency brake on the floorboard that could be applied with the foot. It was on the left side of the floor and easy to apply with one's left foot while using the throttle or the brake with the right foot. All that was required to use it skillfully was to pull the release, mounted under the left dash, with my left hand while driving with the right hand. That gave the driver rear wheel only brakes that made a sliding turn easy to set up. I had done this many times.

I turned the steering wheel slightly to the left as I held the park brake release and simultaneously pressed the park brake with my left foot. I went into a great slide to my right which allowed a tight left hand 180 degree turn. As soon as the rear end was around, I let off the emergency brake, pulled that dual range four speed hydramatic into first gear and hit the throttle. With only half throttle, the tires were spinning on the dirt and helping me complete my turn on the narrow road. I'd done this many times before when alone just for the fun of practicing it. Get the spin momentum going then complete it with the throttle by spinning the rear wheels. The final portion of the turn, on dirt is a matter of letting go of the steering wheel, allowing it to straighten up while applying throttle as necessary to make it happen. It is, actually, very easy to do on the first attempt.

Alva yelled, "Be careful!"

His warning seemed like a misspoken piece of advice. If he wanted us 'careful', then we would be home instead of delivering five gallons of illegal whiskey into the dark. If he desired a cautious way of life, then why indulge in this extremely dangerous career? What he wanted was a driving miracle from a teenage kid. He had chosen the wrong phrase. He wanted 'Luck' not 'Careful'. I knew what we needed. I was ready for the challenge. More than that. I was anxious for the epic chase.

By the time he had finished saying, "Be careful", I was straight in the road, tires spinning and headed the opposite direction. I was feathering the throttle to get as much traction as possible in the dirt. Although the police car I had met was ahead of me, I knew he would turn around to close the trap on us. He was just over the little knoll and I could not see what he was doing. I turned out my lights so that he could not see that I had turned around and was coming at him. I had hit the light switch while turning around in the road. I was pushing and pulling things pretty fast. Brakes, lights, throttle, gears, I was applying all the throttle possible. That wasn't much because this Olds had a lot of torque. The tires were spinning and the road behind me was filled with Arkansas dust. I was struggling to keep it straight. I had ample throttle remaining but couldn't apply more. I topped the knoll in the road and there was the police car right on schedule. I had caught a little air as I topped the knoll. He had just turned around and was headed at me. Lucky for both of us, he had completed the turn around and was headed straight at me and was on his side of the narrow road. Thank God he was on his side the road. My left hand was on the light switch. I was ready. I turned on my lights, bright, as we flashed past each other again. This time I was doing about 60 mph. I am sure he was surprised that I had turned and was facing him so quickly. Unlike him, I had made an unconventional, but much quicker turn around. I was still airborne as we met and my lights came on bright just prior to flashing by him. I was really lucky that he was on his side of the road. With no lights on my car until the last moment, I wonder if he saw me until the moment I flashed by in the air less than two feet from him. It was a narrow road with barely room for two cars side by side. I had as much throttle applied as I could. The road was filled with dust behind me. The sheriff's car disappeared into the dense dust cloud I was creating. I could not see his headlights following me although I knew they would appear soon enough. I had to put as much distance between me and him as possible before he turned around again. I knew I could not outrun his radio. I could only hope to put some distance between us. We needed to dump the whisky. Alva and I had discussed scenarios like this.

Alva said, "Be careful. As soon as you see a good place to pull over, I'll get rid of the whisky. Watch close because I can't see very well to help you out."

I agreed and kept the speed up. We were doing 80 plus with little time to observe speedometer readings. I had reached the terminal velocity on the dirt road. Additional throttle produced no additional speed. It only caused tire spin which caused me to float more on the road. You could hear the rocks hitting the under side the car like hail on a tin roof. I had reached maximum speed for that particular surface. I had my hands full. It was much like driving on an extremely wet surface or ice. The road was straight except for a couple of gentle curves. Mostly it was straight with small knolls hiding what was over the next little hill. I was catching big air on each knoll I topped. I knew the Ridge Road well but we were not back to it and a paved surface yet. Between me and the paved road, there were 4 little knolls. I was counting them. I was counting the times that big Oldsmobile auditioned to become an airplane in the night. It was easy to know when we went airborne. The roar of the rocks hitting the floor would stop abruptly only to begin again as we touched down. It was about 2 miles back to the pavement of the Ridge Road. I knew it in the daytime at lower speeds. At night, and under stressed conditions, I was doubting my counting skill. The paved road was coming up fast but I wasn't sure how soon. At this speed, it was hard to imagine how quickly I would reach it. It was going to come up quick when it did.

I topped the last of the small hills and as the car settled down to the road surface the lights picked up the pavement of the Ridge Road. I let off for the turn, the 90 degree turn I needed to execute. The float was as severe on decel as it was on accel. I seemed to be going the same speed, which was over 80 even when I let off and applied the brakes lightly. All the brakes did was make the vehicle difficult to keep straight in the road. I touched them very lightly. We were still at an excessive speed for a 90 degree turn.

I told Alva, "Hold on tight. We are going to turn."

I think Alva did not see the pavement coming up as early as I did. That only meant he had less time to be frightened. He saw it at the last second. Knowing that I was going to need to pull a miracle out of the hat, I forced the car into a slight left handed attitude in preparation for the turn. Partly skill, partly luck, I was able get the vehicle into nearly a sideways left handed slide on the dirt just before going onto the asphalt. It was a gamble to be sure. I would have prayed for no cross traffic, but I had no time to form the words. While sliding sideways at nearly a 90 degree angle with the dirt road, I pulled that four speed dual range hydramatic transmission into low gear and buried the throttle. The engine was wide open and the tires were spinning as we slid onto the pavement. My timing was good. It was a miracle. It was lots of luck and it was a success. We shot forward, north bound on the Ridge Road like we had been launched from a cannon. The roar from the rocks hitting the floorboard of the car was instantly transformed into a squeal from the rear tires spinning on the asphalt as we hit the paved surface. The side force was so severe as the tires got a bite on the asphalt that both the hubcaps on the right hand side of the car were torn off the wheels from the inertia. I heard them roll out to the side of the road as we accelerated away. The side G's were high. It was an E ticket ride. We were lucky and we were north bound. Most of all, we were upright. I had gained a lot of time on the car behind me. I had also left, unfortunately, two long telltale rubber marks on the asphalt indicating the direction we were headed.

I had the throttle buried. I shifted up and I never lifted until we were well past 100 and some small turns, that I knew well, began to approach. As soon as we recovered from the G forces of the turns I began thinking, "Where can I turn off to dump the whisky?" I was still primarily interested in putting some distance between me and the police car behind me. Could I do that sufficiently so that Alva would have time to dump? Would he need to throw it out the window one at a time?

Alva, almost in answer to my question said, "I'm going to climb over into the back seat to get the sacks in my hand so that I will be ready to dump this as soon as you pull over."

I said, "Good. I will find a place as quick as I can."

I remembered a small turn out that angled off the road and back on. It was access to a rancher's gate, I think. The turn out ran parallel to the road and was about one eighth mile long. It was a smooth, solid, level egress if my memory was accurate. That would be perfect if I could find it in the dark at this speed. The road was familiar, but I had my hands full driving. Lucky again, I saw the spot I needed. I told Alva to get ready. He was already in the back seat. I braked hard while on the paved surface and pulled off the road onto the grassy surface. I had planned for Alva to simply dump the whisky and we would continue. As we slowed on the little road, I saw a big log and mentioned it to Alva. He saw it too.

He said, "Maybe I can set it behind that log."

I came to a stop, Alva was out quickly with the sacks in his hands. He was very agile and strong for his age. He set the sacks behind the log and jumped into the front seat, closing the back door with his hand at the same time.

He said, "I don't think anybody will see it there for days. We might be able to come back and get it depending on how things work out."

Then off the subject somewhat, he said, "I sure like four door cars. They are easy to get in and out of when you're in a hurry."

I never comprehended the irony of his remark in the heat of the chase. I was too busy getting that Olds back up to speed before headlights appeared in the rear view mirror. I made sure the tires weren't spinning when I hit the pavement. Too much throttle and rubber marks would give the car chasing me a nice signature that I had stopped.

Alva said, "Don't go too fast now. There's nothing to worry about."

As much as I enjoyed fast driving, I just wanted to be home. We had failed at the delivery. That was rare. We had succeeded at avoiding capture. That was good. Now, if only I could just be home in my bed. The thought flashed but I knew there was more to do before that reward could be enjoyed.

I took a small dirt road that would eventually lead back to Highway 270. We would be a long way from home but at least we were also a long way from the chase scene.

Alva and I worked our way through the back roads which were all dirt. This was all prior to the advent of helicopters and thermal sensors. Lucky for us. I found a dim log road. I drove up it a ways. We pulled out into the woods without making a sign that we had pulled away from the log road. We stopped, turned off the engine and sat back in the seat. Here we would spend the night and drive out in the morning. No one had seen our car well enough to get a description and certainly not the license number. We got out, shut the doors easily and stood by the car listening. There were no sounds of anyone on the road. We just stood there for a while letting the events soak in.

Finally, Alva said, "That was pretty good driving. You must have been practicing."

I glanced at him and smiled. Sheepishly, I said, "Sometimes."

We drove home the next morning after daylight. We watched carefully as we exited the wooded area because we were still somewhat paranoid regarding the police. No one confronted us. Alva, after days of considering it, decided that returning to the whisky was far to dangerous. He left it behind that log on the Ridge Road. He sacrificed it to the God of Good Luck. We never returned to the scene. Someone eventually stumbled onto five gallons of good whisky. I never knew the outcome.

CHAPTER FORTY NINE

First Job

I gave a few of my friends rides to school in my car.

It didn't take long before I realized that having a car was great, but having money to buy some gas so that you could go somewhere was even better. Alva gave me money to buy gas to go to school. Gas was cheap. It was about 30 cents per gallon. Even so, school used up the one or two dollars per week that Alva gave me. There was no fuel to go anywhere else. It was time to get a job. This would be another first.

One of my friends (one who rode to school with me daily) worked at the local newspaper, The Malvern Daily Record. One day he said, "They want someone to sweep up and empty trash at the newspaper. Would you want to do that?"

I said, "Sure".

Maybe I had me a job. My friend's name was Robert. He took me with him to work on the following Saturday. I was introduced to the owner, Mrs. Francis Beerstecher. Pronounced, *best-ter-shay*. She was a feisty little woman who hired me immediately and later became my friend. The pay was 50 cents per hour. I was happy to get it.

This was my first job. I swept floors and emptied trash cans. I worked one hour before school and arrived at school shortly after 8 AM. I gave a few of my friends rides to school in my car. I worked three hours after school and gave one my friends a ride home after work. I worked all day on Saturday. I accumulated about 28 hours per week, normally. That's $14.00 minus deductions. In today's money, that's about $140 per week while going to school full time. It helped tremendously with purchases of food and gas. I made decent passing grades. I could have done better. I wish I had made a better effort toward high grades. At the time, I saw no need. That was dumb. Performing adequately is not good enough. One should always attempt to excel. I'm sorry to say I learned that lesson much later.

Robert and I became traveling partners. He worked the same hours that I did only he had no car. I've forgotten why Robert never drove. I think he may have lost his license for some reason. Either way, we never discussed it. He never had a car. We went everywhere in my car. Robert began a career in the Navy after high school. Robert was the same age as I but one grade behind me. I've never kept in contact with him.

Alva was intermittently civil with me. I think he was glad to have me living at our house and acting as a caretaker of it. Sometimes when he was home and there was no whisky to tend to he would ask me to ride along as we went to another town. Sometimes I would go just to break the boredom. Plus, it saved my gasoline.

Alva spent a lot of time with his girlfriend in Hot Springs. I spent a lot of time alone. A friend of mine, Doyle Holyfield, lived alone with his father and brother, Bobby. We spent a lot of time together. Doyle always had his own truck or car. I had a car, but I wished I had a brother like Doyle. I especially wished for one like Doyle's brother, Bobby. Bobby sided with me once when I was bullied by an older kid. I've never forgotten that favor.

CHAPTER FIFTY

The Final Whipping

It was dark and I could taste the blood in my mouth.

Often when I was living primarily alone on Babcock Street, I would grow bored with only reading and staying alone. During one of those many occasions I decided to go visit my Aunt Dora. She lived about 12 miles away and was still living in the same house that my Mother had escaped to on the night that Alva shot at her. Alva had not been home for more than a week. I was unsure when he would come back. It was Saturday evening and I had gotten off work earlier. So, with no telephone or other communication, I decided to leave a note for Alva on the dinning table announcing where I was going and when I'd be back. I said in the note that I'd be back on Sunday evening, one day later. I'd planned to spend the night with Aunt Dora and Harold, her son, and watch some television with them. We had no television or radio at our house.

I wrote a note, left it open on the dining table with a glass holding it down, then got into my little black Chevy and drove to Dora's house. I was about 15 years old. Dora and Harold were glad to see me. They asked where Alva was. I had to tell them that I didn't know and hadn't seen him for a week. They made no comment. We settled down for an evening of TV. There were only 2 channels. I had done this before and it was enjoyable to me. Dora and Harold were family and seemed like it. They always appeared to enjoy my company. I was happy to be with them.

After all the TV shows had signed off, which was about midnight, I went to bed in one of their bedrooms. Dora's house was simple but she always kept everything very clean. It was a clean country house. Apparently, Alva came home to Babcock Street about midnight or shortly after on the same day that I left. He looked for me but couldn't find me. I was gone. My car was gone. He was perplexed at his failure to find me at home. He never bothered to look on the table for a note. The dining table was where we had always left notes for each other through the years. He went into one of his rages for which he was famous. Apparently, after considerable looking and driving to my friend Doyle's house to ask about me, he decided to drive up to Dora's house. It was now about 3 AM. Upon seeing my car there his anger increased. He couldn't stand to know that I had gone anywhere without his approval although there was no way to contact him for a week, or possibly more, prior to this. He expected me to be at home any time he showed up no matter how long the intervals were between appearances. That was unreasonable, but it was his expectation. Since I had not abided by his expectations, I was in trouble. That meant I paid with a beating.

After he exhausted his search near our home, he decided to drive to Dora's home to continue the search. Upon his arrival at Dora's, he burst into the house and found me asleep in the bed. My first recollection of the event was as he jerked me from the bed by my hair. I awoke when he jerked me out of bed by my hair and literally threw me against the opposing wall. I awoke while in midair. I fully remember hitting the wall. It was like an automobile wreck. I was half conscious due to a combination of the impact and sleep. It was dark and I could taste the blood in my mouth. I don't know if he hit me first or if the crash into the wall caused the mouth injury. Either way, there was plenty of blood and cursing and screaming. I was doing the bleeding part and trying to get up as he kicked me around the floor and slapped me down each time I tried to get up. Dora was yelling at him to stop, but he paid no attention. He was in his rage. Later I learned from Aunt Dora that she had, after failing to stop Alva's entry, gone to get Harold who slept in a third bedroom. Harold was a deep sleeper and had not awakened at the first sounds.

After several slaps and kicks, I can't count how many, Alva had worn himself down. I had last landed in a corner farthest from the door in which he stood. Dora had now turned on the lights in the hallway. It was dark in the room where I was with light spilling in from the adjacent room. Alva stood silhouetted in the door way to the bedroom. I was hurting all over. My head still hurt from hitting the wall. My mouth hurt and blood was still flowing from where one of my teeth had punctured my lip. My butt hurt from all the kicks. Harold had finally gotten up and was yelling at Alva from somewhere else in the house as he put on his pants. I could hear all the sounds. I knew nothing could stop him but fatigue once he was on a roll. Right now he was blocking the door and resting up for the next round. I'd seen this before. It was all too familiar to me. When I was a kid in the briar patch, I was scared so badly, beaten so thoroughly, that I soiled my pants. On this night, I was not the little kid in the briar patch. Alva was beating me but I was not beaten. This time was different.

I was scared but inside there was something that said, "That's enough." That voice said, "You have done nothing to deserve this beating. So, end it."

I had no weapon. I was unsure if even Harold could stop him. I didn't know how much longer he would beat me. I knew that all poor Dora could do was try to talk him back into his senses. While he stood there panting and getting his second wind so that he could begin on me again, I lay crumpled in the far corner of the room. From where I retrieved the idea is unknown. It came from desperation and fear and it came, maybe, from courage, if I had any at that point. However it came, it did come. I had to say something. I had to do something to stop him from hitting me again. I didn't want to be hit again.

I raised one bloody index finger in the air. I didn't point the finger at him. I simply raised it in the air. It took me a minute to get my breath because several of those kicks had caught me at the belt line and knocked the breath out of me. So, I raised that finger in the air and it remained there dramatically while I sucked in a lung full of air. I wanted all the air I could take in so that I could get a sentence out without hesitating.

I said, finally, a few words at a time, "If you hit me again, you'd better kill me, because if you don't, I will kill you. This finger, this bloody finger can pull a trigger just a well as yours and I will use that finger to pull a trigger to kill you if you hit me again."

I kept the finger in the air like it was going to stop him. I had nothing but determination on my side. I certainly had plenty of that and it was building as I spoke. Alva's life rested in his next move. Perhaps mine also. Perhaps he sensed the gravity of the moment.

Alva listened. He said nothing. Harold and Dora heard it also. Beat up, from the floor, I had gotten his attention. There was no sound from anyone except the sound of hard breathing. I was unsure if he was going to start on me again. Whether he did or not, I had meant exactly what I had said. As I sat there, second by second, I became less afraid of the consequences of my threat. I was dead serious. In that moment that those words came from my mouth, I ceased to be the beaten boy. I have not experienced fear since that night. I was never afraid of physical violence after that. It was a turning point for me, forever. I don't view myself as courageous. I simply ran completely out of fear that night and tapped into something else. I became personally acquainted with Determination. For the remainder of my life, Determination has protected me from Fear. I was not and still am not proud of what I said. I have revealed this night to only a couple of people until now. I would not want my epithet to be 'the one who threatened his father's life'. No matter, that event happened. I didn't set the event into motion. However, my determination ended it. Forever afterward my thought processes were altered by that event. In those few seconds I stopped being a boy. I grew up years in that long moment in the dark corner of Aunt Dora's house. As long as it has been, a feeling of sadness overwhelms me when I think of it.

After a long straight look, Alva turned, said nothing to anyone, exited the room, got into his car and drove away. I did not see Alva at our house on Babcock Street for a month. He never mentioned the event to me again. I never mentioned it other than to show him the note that I had left on the table when he finally came home a month later.

I held the note up and said, "Here's the note that you didn't see."

He looked at it but didn't answer. He never mentioned it again.

Dora and Harold tried as well as they could to wash me up and console me after Alva had left. Dora helped me wash my face and encouraged me to wash my mouth with something that stung the cut. I had a few injuries that took a while to heal. My lip was punctured through to the outside from my tooth. One tooth was chipped which eventually wore away smooth. Other than being stiff and sore I survived it all pretty well.

We stayed up until nearly dawn talking. Dora said that Alva had always had a temper. She said that older kids had picked on him a lot when he was very young. She thought that was why he had such a violent temper. She said he was more sensitive to hazing type behavior from older kids than some of the other kids were. She thought that made a difference in his attitude. Dora said Alva kept to himself a lot as a kid. She believed it was because he couldn't tolerate the constant harassment by older kids. Alva had revealed to me that he always had to wear the hand me down clothes of all the other kids because he was the youngest boy. Alva, more than once, had revealed to me his clothes were filled with patches. I knew this much. I remember him saying that he had "patches on the patches" sometimes. Other kids laughed and poked fun at his clothes and that bothered him deeply. He said some called him "Patches" because of his clothes. He told me that and wept as he told me.

Dora said Alva's first wife Violet was very nice and pretty too. She was surprised when they divorced after many years of marriage. She thought they were happy. Dora said she had no knowledge of him being violent with Violet or their children. That corresponded to scraps of information Alva had revealed to me during fits of anger.

His description was, "I never had to get mad at Violet and the girls like I had to at you and your Mother."

I believe there was a message in that statement that revealed something about him. I could never put the puzzle pieces together in a way that explained his violent behavior with my Mother and me. But underneath his calm exterior, he held an unwarranted vendetta for my Mother and me. It seemed so.

After getting patched up and eating a nice breakfast the next morning with Dora and Harold, I drove my Chevy home on Sunday afternoon. My typical Sunday afternoon was comprised of getting all my homework in order for the next morning, washing some clothes, shining my shoes and doing my ironing. I'm sure that is what I did on this particular Sunday afternoon when I arrived home. Afterwards, I would, typically, read for a while. I usually read until midnight. It was not uncommon for me to fall asleep in my rocking chair which was in the middle of our front room.

I always awoke at 5:30 AM. I would attend to my personal hygiene then cook my breakfast which was two eggs, bacon and biscuits which I made from scratch. I made hot chocolate to accompany the eggs and bacon. I really enjoyed those breakfasts. I still enjoy them, occasionally. I did it the same every morning. So, I became fast, with all the practice. After finishing with my dish washing, I would get into my car, pick up my friend, Robert, and we would go to work at the newspaper at 7 AM for an hour before school. The bell rang for the first class about 8:20 AM. This routine was characteristic for every day except Sunday. Of course, there was no school on Saturday so, I worked all day. I was never absent from school. I always had my homework on time. I made decent grades. I asked for nothing from anyone. I was forced to be responsible for myself. I hated the process at times, but it forged me into a person who can take care of himself and others. For that, I'm grateful.

CHAPTER FIFTY ONE

Leaving Home

After the last physical encounter with Alva, our relationship declined even more. He, when home, continually stated that he wanted me to leave as soon as I graduated from school. I told him I would. I had established a writing relationship with my Mother in Shreveport, Louisiana. We had exchanged a few letters. She had offered to allow me live there while I worked with her husband, Don. My plans were to finish school, then move there. I had saved enough money from my newspaper job to finance my trip.

Shortly after my graduation I packed my clothes and moved to my Mother's home in Shreveport. It was my last time to live under my father's roof. Although we had our rough times, he was there for my departure. He waved good bye and had tears in his eyes as I drove away. So did I.

Conclusions and Acknowledgments

At the time of this writing, I'm 69, nearly 70 years old. I've been married a couple of times. The second one, 25 years, worked better than the first. I'm currently single. I live alone in my home and I'm completely at peace with myself. I love my books and my tools, my computers and my cameras. Most of all, I love my family and the friends I have made. I'm alone but never lonely. I have many interests which I pursue as though they were my livelihood. Among those are automobiles, photography, videography, computers, writing, hunting, and saltwater fishing. I'm always reading. My day job for the past 26 years, is the management and operation of my business where we repair and construct collectible classic American automobiles. I love it. My 'Peace' is defined as: A love of Life and the acceptance of the inevitable prospect of Death. Although there are many things I wish to have done differently, I do not lay awake at night worrying about those things and what might have been. I make sincere attempts to view life through the windshield rather than the rear view mirror. This essay is the only exception. I've become reasonably good at it. I try to affect the future and give the past an honorable burial.

As a result of the experiences I encountered and documented here, I learned to read well early in life. I read rapidly and easily retain most of it. That was a great attribute to acquire early. Reading has been entertaining and it has benefitted me tremendously throughout my life. I attribute it to the lack of a radio and television. I had no other ways to entertain myself. The absence of other media, combined with hours of loneliness likely worked to my advantage by forcing me to read. Thanks again go to Alva for noticing my interest in reading. His gift, when I was 10, of a set of World Book Encyclopedia was an entertaining and educational asset to have in my home. Once when I had grown tired of the library books, I began reading the World Books. I read each one, as if it were a novel, until I completed the set of 19 volumes. That included the supplement volume. It took several months. I failed to thank Alva properly after I grew older and acquired thoughts more sophisticated than I possessed in 1954 at the time of the gift. I'm sorry for my failure to thank him for those encyclopedia. He often saw me reading them and was happy with his initial decision to purchase the set.

Those described experiences forced me to learn to drive early. I drove well long before my friends who were often older than I. Hand/eye coordination necessary for driving was developed very early. As a result, I drive easily and smoothly without stress whether I'm in an 18 wheeled tractor trailer or a race car. Statistics show that kids who learn tasks that require good hand/eye coordination, also tasks like a second language are benefitted greatly by learning them very early in life. I owe many of my skills to being forced to learn them early.

In addition, I acquired the ability to size up a new acquaintance instantly and easily. Largely, this ability was helped along by my encounters with a very wide variety of personalities. It became like a sixth sense. I can't explain it. It's just there.

Liars stand out from the crowd like a bad odor. I do it unconsciously, without thinking. That has helped me greatly during my role as a manager of a business and as the owner/manager of my business. This is hardly unique. I have numerous friends who exhibit this *ability*. It has honed my 'street smarts' like a fine stone puts an edge to good steel.

'What does not kill me makes me stronger' were quoted by the German philosopher Friedrich Wilhelm Nietzsche (October 15, 1844 – August 25, 1900). I can testify to the accuracy of his quote.

The writing of this essay has caused me to experience many emotions. I am surprised at the deep feelings aroused by my sojourn into my past. Among them are sadness, love, anger, joy, humor and sometimes lengthy bouts of melancholy. Many of those emotions I have experienced at a much greater level than I believed I would prior to my beginning this project. It was difficult at times to continue with the story. It was more difficult to leave it unfinished once I began. Most of all, telling it has set me free without my realization of the transformation until it was finished. It has been very therapeutic. I have needed to do it for me, but I did not know that when I began it. No longer do I have to keep the damn secrets.

After spending many years thinking about the events that transpired during my period at home as a participant and as a child growing up while in the middle of activities that were considered off limits by most, I have tried to assimilate that period into the balance of my life. By writing this essay, I have attempted to reveal events and the feelings and thoughts that coursed through me as the events were happening around me. I wanted to share it with others which is the direct opposite of my motivation throughout my childhood. I was encouraged to share my experiences by close friends to whom I revealed bits and pieces. Donna Nichols/Blair, my classmate, my long time friend, was very influential. Donna lit my fire of determination with a few effective words during our 50th class reunion in Malvern, Arkansas. I'm happy that she did this. Thank you very much for your nagging, Donna. Donna and her sister, Judy Walters, the author of ***"How It Was and Is for Me",*** each experienced traumatic upbringings. All, in some fashion, related to alcohol. Hearing and reading each of their stories individually, finally inspired me to tell this segment of mine. Thanks go to Nanci Achzehner/Burris for the tremendous editing skills she applied to my final version of this book. Without the hours she spent on my 'finished copy', my mistakes would have been exposed to the world.

Many thanks go to Ian Guy for the artistry that produced the cover image, originally, a 20 X 16 oil painting named, *Moonshine Runner*, for ***Moonshine***. Ian lives in the UK. He is a professional and produces numerous and attractive images of motoring art. He originally produced this image, the oil painting, for an American customer who restored and owns the actual vehicle, a 1938 Chevrolet coupe, named *Shaky Lady*. The coupe was a real life moonshine runner complete with a hidden tank and a tap under the rear bumper for draining the contents. Treat yourself to some fantastic automotive art by visiting his web site, www.motoringartist.com. You will be excited and surprised. Ian Guy can be reached, by email, at ianguy@motoringartist.com.

The composition of this essay is not a pretense to psychoanalyze myself. I'll leave that to professionals. Neither is this an attempt at an autobiography. This is only a segment of life, mine, that pertained to alcohol. I want this story to console and verify the lives of others who may have thought they were the only ones. I know I'm not the only kid who was caught up in such activities. However, by telling my story, I hope to produce a stabilizing effect on others who have experienced similar events in their life. Also, I want my children to know the things I never talk about. Perhaps, although things of this nature didn't happen to you directly, you may more easily understand the behavior of a close friend or a mate who had something of this type happen to them. If so, encourage them to talk about it. Help to set them free.

It's a strange, torn feeling that, even now, I find difficult to describe. I find it impossible to express my feelings with a single emotion about this era of my life. I felt abandoned. I felt used. I sometimes felt loved. I didn't feel particularly neglected, but I did feel suppressed. Stifled sometimes. I often felt abused but, strangely, that physically abused feeling, the severe whippings, didn't hurt as deeply as the feeling of abandonment. That was the real abuse. I've been unable to overcome the feeling of abandonment that reared into life at that time. The feeling of abandonment has seasoned nearly everything I have done in life. I realize that, now. I often, justifiably, felt unwanted. I was frequently told by Alva that my Mother was a whore and I was not his kid. He would frequently resort, when angry, to telling me that he was crazy to have stayed and helped raise me. Amazingly, after I was an adult and after our fences were mended between us, he would reflect on how much I resembled him at the same age. Another paradox. I sometimes felt needed while often, simultaneously, felt that I was in the way and unwanted. I was told, directly, by Alva that I was in the way and unwanted. Most of all, I felt that I'd been prevented from just being a kid. I needed, as most healthy kids, in order to develop evenly, to feel carefree much of the time. I *never* felt carefree while growing up. I felt very restricted. I had to keep many secrets. I was asked, frequently, with only a moment's notice, to verify that I was properly keeping the secrets. The interrogations were almost daily up until about 10 years old. If the response I gave was unsatisfactory, then a strong whipping quickly followed. After the whipping the interrogation was repeated until I answered Alva's questions as he thought I should. Sometimes, it took multiple whippings before I figured out the word combination Alva wished to hear. Always, I felt I was on a powder keg ready to blow if I behaved or spoke incorrectly. I had dreams, as a child, about powder kegs with lit fuses, ready to blow. This had to result from the stressful situation under which I lived. I have raised my three children to feel personal responsibility while making every attempt to allow them to feel carefree. That was my goal. They can answer how well I achieved that goal. In my opinion, they have all turned out marvelous. One could say, I've tried to set a standard for them that differed from the one with which I was reared.

Alva was never arrested for making or selling whisky. His arrests were all for acts of violence against someone. He was never arrested for acts of violence against his family although many were committed. He never apologized to any of his family for the violent things he did. He said, to me, many times that he was never required to spank his two girls, ever. Yet, he found it 'necessary' to beat me, severely, many times. Nearly all the beatings were far beyond the scope of average discipline.

Alva told me of many instances when living in hotels and overhearing conflicts in the adjoining room, he had gone to the rescue of a kid who was being spanked too harshly. However, he beat me far more harshly than the kid he reportedly rescued. Alva had a dual code of ethics. By the same token, his immediate family was allowed to escape criticism when they committed acts that he would condemn when others did the identical thing. It seemed that if he liked you, then you could do nothing wrong. If he disliked you, then you could do nothing right. He was not above making one feel his dislike physically. While I was a kid, I felt that my Mother and I were severely disliked. After I was an adult and had been separated from Alva for years, a metamorphosis of opinion blessed me. He decided that I could do no wrong. Perhaps that meant that he began liking me. I hope that was the case although he never voiced it.

Alva was artistically inclined. He loved classical music, blues and, of course, his Irish Jigs. He loved the violin and banjo. He was creatively inspired and was great at visualization. For instance, he enjoyed looking at the clouds and imagining images formed by them. Nearly every random design in the stars, clouds, or designs in the bark of a tree caused him to imagine an animal or human image. Sometimes the imagines made him recall old friends, long gone. Memories of those aroused emotions within him. He told great stories and enjoyed reading or writing poetry. He was very patriotic. He could memorize poems easily. It is shameful that these attributes failed to be noticed and encouraged when he was young.

I divorced my first wife due to her inappropriate behavior. She was the mother of my two daughters, Tammy and Dawn. My absence caused my two girls to confront greater responsibilities, greater challenges than they might have had I been there. Each, unknown to me at the time, was subjected to unspeakable acts of sexual abuse in my absence. In view of that knowledge, I constantly ponder the justification for my absence. Even more of the credit for their development reflects on the tenacity of each of them when confronted with personal challenges after my divorce from their Mother. Each has molded them self into a responsible, caring lady with a great career and a well bonded family. My attempts to visit my children while they were 'incarcerated' by their Mother and the new step-dad was met with clever refusals and avoidance. The step-dad behaved in ways with my daughters, if revealed while he was alive, would have sent him to prison permanently. Had I known of his behavior, my response would have surely sent me to prison permanently. Neither Tammy, Dawn, nor I, have fully recovered from that period of time prior to the day the step-dad was fried by high voltage as he attempted to lower a radio antenna. The step-dad's death by electrocution ended his siege on my daughters' innocence.

During my second marriage to Nanci and the rearing of our son, Jason, I was fully present for his development from the moment of his birth until he left home for his first try at living alone. That turned out extremely well. He is now happily married with a great career and a wonderful new son. Jason has earned my deep admiration. My goal was always to allow all of my children more carefree moments than I experienced. I did that to the best of my ability. I was reasonably successful.

Kids should to be allowed to be kids for a while. The hard stuff comes soon enough.

I welcome your comments.

moonshinebook1@gmail.com

www.moonshinebook.com

About Grant Burris

Grant moved from Arkansas to California when he was about 19 years old. At that time he was married and had a daughter who was 3 months old. In California he worked at a Buick dealership for 22 years. During that 22 year span he took a break for 2 years, bought a large motor home and toured the entire United States with his wife, Nanci. In 1988 he purchased an auto repair business named, the Tune Up Shop. He has owned and operated that business in Costa Mesa, California for 27 years after transforming it into a premier classic car and hot rod shop. He has commented frequently regarding how stress free his career is. I have heard him say, "I can't wait to get to work in the mornings."